EXPOSED:

THE FINANCIAL
MATRIX

New York Times Best-Selling Author
ORRIN WOODWARD

The information presented in this book is for general educational purposes only, and provides information the authors believe to be accurate on the subject matter covered. It is sold with the understanding that neither the authors nor the publisher are providing advice for any particular portfolio or for any individual's particular situation, or rendering investment advice or other professional services such as legal or accounting advice. If expert assistance in areas that include investment, legal, and accounting advice are needed, please seek a competent professional's services.

This publication may make reference to performance data collected over various periods of time. Remember that past results do not guarantee future performance. Performance data, as well as laws and regulations, change over time, which could affect the applicability of the information presented in this book. Any data presented herein is used merely to illustrate the underlying principles.

This book is not to serve as the basis for any financial decision or as a recommendation of any specific investment.

No warranty is made with respect to the accuracy or completeness of the information contained herein, and both the authors and the publisher specifically disclaim any responsibility for any liability, loss, or risk, personal or otherwise, which is incurred as a consequence, directly or indirectly, of the use and application of any of the contents of this book.

Published by:

Obstaclés Press
200 Commonwealth Court
Cary, NC 27511

orrinwoodward.com

ISBN: 978-0-9990440-8-7

First Edition, December 2020
10 9 8 7 6 5 4 3 2 1

Scripture quotations marked "KJV" are taken from The Holy Bible, Cambridge, 1769.

Scripture quotations marked "NIV" are taken from The Holy Bible, New International Version®, NIV®, Copyright© 1973, 1978, 1984, 2011 by Biblica, Inc.® Used by permission of Biblica, Inc.® All rights reserved worldwide.

Printed in the United States of America

If you do nothing else with this book,
at least read this page.

You may have felt the financial system is rigged.

It is.

You may have felt the financial system is taking
advantage of you.

It is.

You may have wondered if there is
anything you can do about it.

There is.

This book will show you how.

CONTENTS

FOREWORD

Congratulations on picking up this book. I guarantee you have never read anything like it. What follows in these pages is jolting, thoroughly researched, and painstakingly reasoned out. At first it may even strike you as a bit out-of-the-blue, especially when compared to the issues the national media and other gatekeepers of information flow seem intent on making our priority. As you will discover, this is no accident. The very fact that we hardly hear anything at all about what you are about to read screams loudly for its validity. As the saying goes, "The greatest trick the Devil ever played was convincing the world he didn't exist."

Make no mistake; what you are about to learn is indeed very real, and it affects all of us in meaningful ways every day. This book will show you that. It will uncover and document systemic plunder and rampant unfairness. Like an engrossing Agatha Christie mystery, it will expose an insidious plot and explain the crime with several "smoking guns" of evidence, taking you deeper and deeper with one stunning reveal after another. By the end you will view money and the economy, and especially your own particular financial situation, in an entirely new and unexpected way. In short, you will be changed. You will have a new perspective and arrive irreversibly at a new place. To borrow from the 1999 hit movie *The Matrix,* as does this book, you will have taken the "red pill" and learned life-changing truth. The financial world will never so readily fool you again.

As with all information, however, one must always ask, "Who says?" The credibility of the messenger must be proportional to the magnitude of the message. And that's the other astonishing thing about this book; it very likely could not nor would not have been written by anyone else. Orrin Woodward writes as Marco Polo returning from a journey to a distant and unknown land, as having "been there" and experienced it all firsthand. Growing up in a blue-collar home in a tiny rural village in Michigan, Woodward was out of the house at age eighteen and paid his own way through college, often living on a few dollars a week. He had no family wealth, connections, prospects, sponsors, patrons, or even fans. But somehow in approximately a decade and a half, he had won national engineering awards, built several successful businesses, become a millionaire many times over, written *New York Times* best-selling books, been listed in *Inc. Magazine's* Top 20 Leaders in the world, and even set a Guinness Book World Record. It was precisely this journey from obscurity to notoriety and fortune that taught him the main thesis of this book: the financial system is intentionally rigged against the unsuspecting masses of people who strive futilely within it. If Woodward had not struggled so mightily himself to rise up and climb the slippery slope from lower middle class to the 0.5% income earners and beyond, he would never have seen it. Further, he would not have had the freedom to invest the thousands of required hours of study and research to gain the insights and find the evidence for what is here presented. Finally, Woodward's broad knowledge and experience as an engineer, entrepreneur, consultant, counselor, writer, speaker, world traveler, international business owner, investor, theologian, philanthropist, economist, and all-around modern polymath make him uniquely qualified and positioned to sound this clarion call.

The message of this book is important, timely, and necessary. What happens as a result of its publication could be hugely important for mankind and the world's economy, but even more so, for you. Read on and don't miss a thing, and prepare to "see" many things for the first time, anew.

Chris Brady
New York Times #1 Best-Selling Author
Cary, NC

The Financial Matrix

The 1999 movie *The Matrix*[1] portrayed a system-of-control that captured human energy to power an artificial intelligence (AI) computer system controlling the world. Although it was a science fiction thriller, the movie depicted reality in many ways. The only difference is that the system-of-control over human energy is not AI computers, but instead the modern financial system.

The parallels between the current financial system and the fictional movie were so striking I named the Financial Matrix in its honor. After all, the global financial monopoly enjoys unlimited profits and power through siphoning the people's wealth similar to *The Matrix* AI computers siphoning the people's energy. Several scenes from the movie, in fact, can be quoted verbatim about the Financial Matrix, including when Morpheus explained to Neo how the Matrix was a system-of-control:

> That system is our enemy. But when you're inside, you look around, what do you see? Businessmen, teachers, lawyers, carpenters. The very minds of the people we are trying to save. But until we do, these people are still a part of that system . . . not ready to be unplugged. And many of them are so inured, so

hopelessly dependent on the system that they will fight to protect it.

This book exposes the Financial Matrix because it has thrived on ignorance, having "pulled the wool over the people's eyes, blinding them to the truth." That ends today. Enslavement by the Financial Matrix is not right, as Morpheus warned Neo in *The Matrix*:

> That you are a slave, Neo. Like everyone else, you were born into bondage, born into a prison that you cannot smell or taste or touch. A prison . . . for your mind. . . . Unfortunately, no one can be . . . told what the [Financial] Matrix is. . . . You have to see it for yourself.

Morpheus placed two pills in front of Neo: take the blue pill and remain in blissful ignorance serving the Matrix, or take the red pill and learn the truth, "no matter how deep the rabbit hole goes," by joining the team intent on exposing and escaping the Matrix. Neo chose the red pill, pursuing uncomfortable truths to be set free, rather than comfortable lies which would keep him in bondage. I offer the reader the same choices pertaining to the Financial Matrix: take the blue pill and live in illusions and bondage, or take the red pill and learn the truth to set yourself free. For those who choose the red pill, this book will expose the truth about the Financial Matrix and teach the people of the world how to escape.

Edmund Burke once said: "All that is necessary for the triumph of evil is that good men [and women] do nothing."[2] The people have been financially plundered long enough. However, we cannot defeat injustice with further injustices. After all, darkness cannot scatter darkness. To change the financial system, we must follow Buckminster Fuller's advice: "You never change things by fighting the existing reality. In order to change something, you need to build a new model that makes the existing one obsolete."[3]

It's time to make the Financial Matrix obsolete. It's time for the world to learn what it is, how it works, and how to escape the Financial Matrix. Above all, it's time to restore financial justice, setting the people free to enjoy their God-given rights and responsibilities to life, liberty, and property.

This would be a much better world if more married couples were as deeply in love as they are in debt.

—Earl Wilson

The Truth Will Set You Free

"But Orrin, you promised me." These words, although spoken nearly thirty years ago, still stir my soul today. After all, my lovely bride had just called me out. And, despite my rationalizations, she was right. I had promised Laurie she could be a stay-at-home mom once we started our family, but now that the moment was upon us, I was hesitating. If we could barely cover our bills with both of us working, how were we going to make it on one income? I was paralyzed. Do I follow my heart and fulfill my promise to Laurie, or follow my head and fulfill our financial obligations?

In reality, my conundrum started months earlier, when Laurie announced we were pregnant. Whoa! Talk about mixed emotions, as the joy of starting our family battled the fear of economic uncertainty for emotional supremacy. Nonetheless, I simply ignored the cognitive dissonance and celebrated with Laurie. The next day, however, the fears returned. Why was I so troubled? Well, for one thing, my parents had taught me to keep my word. For another, our finances were a mess, and even with both of us employed (as an engineer and accountant), we had accumulated over $32,000 of debt, not including our mortgage. Furthermore, we didn't have much room to cut back financially, as we weren't living high on the hog in a ranch house of less than one thousand square feet and driving used vehicles.

I had no idea how to both keep my promise and stay afloat financially, especially once the baby's expenses were added and my wife's salary subtracted. Absurdly, like an ostrich burying its head in the sand, I refused to confront reality, as if ignoring it would somehow make the problem disappear. Even more alarming, I had convinced myself that Laurie enjoyed accounting so much that she intended to continue working after our baby was born. I was procrastinating, hoping my supportive spouse would do similarly. Fortunately for us, she had other plans.

My delusions were shattered on a warm spring night, shortly before heading to Ann Arbor for another MBA class, when Laurie asked when she should give her two weeks' notice. Bewildered by her boldness, I quickly rehashed excuses about poor finances, poor timing, and the importance of her income. She listened, but when I was done, she simply shook her head and said, "Orrin, you promised me." While I couldn't deny the truthfulness of her statement, I attempted to deflect its impact by suggesting a delayed implementation plan. Again, she merely shook her head and repeated, "Orrin, you promised me." Facts are pesky things, and no matter where I sought shelter, those pesky facts hounded me. The irrefutable truths of her message were breaking through my rationalizations as I mumbled incoherently one more time. It was all for nought, however, because she paused, looked me in the eyes and directly into my soul, and stated once again, "But Orrin, you promised me." That was it—game, set, and match to Laurie Woodward. The truth was about to set us free!

In retrospect, I now realize Laurie believed in me more than I believed in myself. The analysis paralysis was over, and although the financial challenge remained, the character issue was resolved. I had made a promise, and I intended to keep it. That night, the drive to Ann Arbor was filled with questions, questions that led to the discovery of the Financial Matrix. Where did we go wrong financially? Didn't we do everything *they* said to do: go to the best schools, get the best grades, and enter the best professions? Be that as it may, we were still living paycheck to paycheck. The American Dream felt out of reach, and despite many achievements (multiple honor societies, four US patents, the youngest senior engineer in my building, and a national technical benchmarking award all by age twenty-five), the truth of the matter was I could not provide for my family. And, if the definition of insanity is continuing to do the same thing while expecting a different result, then I was definitely bordering on financial insanity.

To be sure, I wanted our financial results to change, but I kept doing the same things. No matter how hard I worked or how many classes I took, I was not getting ahead financially. New results demand the application of new information, and I vowed to get new information from those who had achieved the results we desired. One of the biggest breakthroughs was to approach success with the same systematic rigor that I applied to manufacturing processes at work. For instance, engineers make predictions and then run designed experiments to confirm them, believing, "In God we trust; all others must have data." This was standard operating procedure for work, but it never occurred to me to apply it to life.

From now on, Laurie and I would apply the same engineering rigor to the important areas of life we sought to improve. Timeless success habits are not hidden and are readily discoverable to those who are seeking. After all, success leaves clues, and people who create success in a free market have vision, belief, and habits that produce consistent results. The key to going through a minefield, therefore, is to follow the footsteps of someone who has made it to the other side successfully. The Bible says you will know them by their fruit, and we applied this financially by no longer accepting advice without properly checking the fruit on the tree of the person providing the advice. Financial mentors, in other words, can only guide you as far as they have gone because to claim to know, but not to do, is not to know.

John Wayne once said, "Life is tough, even tougher when you are stupid," and I was done being financially stupid, blindly following the blind. Accordingly, Laurie and I focused on finding people with the results we wanted and becoming hungry and disciplined students to apply the success clues. In less than a decade, we went from a financial mess to financial freedom, creating monthly incomes surpassing the combined annual incomes of our former jobs. We now live the life we've always wanted, and our wealth has continued to snowball because we built our financial foundation on the rock of debt-free ownership, instead of the sand of debt payments.

This is not said boastfully, but gratefully, in thankfulness for the Grace of God, the inspiring models we followed, and the powerful principles we learned. I pray this book raises the bar for you like Laurie's conversation raised the bar for me. I cannot emphasize enough how effective the financial principles are when applied consistently. They worked in the past, they work in the present, and they will work in the future. The only question is, will the reader work to apply them? It's time to share our journey of discovery, a journey fueled by hunger and vision, that led to new beliefs and habits, which produced new results. This book is a road map through the minefield, a step-by-step guide to financial justice, helping you to live the life you've always wanted.

Rather go to bed supperless, than rise in debt.

—BENJAMIN FRANKLIN

CHAPTER 1

Debts, Inflation, and Compound Interest

The world is drowning in debt. Over the last fifty years, total debts have ballooned to unimaginable levels worldwide, surpassing by multiple orders of magnitude anything previously experienced in history. Something is amiss. While sounding the alarm, however, I don't intend to sound pessimistic or leave readers without hope. Instead, this chapter emphasizes that debt is not natural, it is a form of bondage, and one should not enter into it without due consideration. After all, the key to the financial elites' profits and control is debt, as Ezra Pound noted: "Wars in old times were made to get slaves. The modern implement of imposing slavery is debt."[1] And our world is being enslaved in debt, with the United States of America, dismally, leading the charge.

I will share the American debt data because it is readily available. However, I encourage readers to study the debt data for their respective countries also, as most are similarly in debt. According to the 2019 Federal Reserve data (this is before the further multitrillions added during the COVID-19 pandemic), American debt was $53 trillion. This total was broken down into three main categories:[2]

American Total Debts: $53 trillion

1. Household Debts: $15.8 trillion
2. Business Debts: $15.7 trillion
3. Government Debts: $21.4 trillion

Worse yet, this doesn't take into account the federal IOUs on liabilities for such things as Social Security, Medicare, and federal and military benefits for which no money has been set aside. When all of these are added together, the total unfunded liabilities surpass $122 trillion. This indicates that America's federal government must raise over $175 trillion just to get back to breakeven. For a point of reference, the total size of the American economy, the gross domestic product (GDP), is only $21 trillion, which indicates that the federal government's commitments are more than eight times larger than the total economy. And the total American debts and unfunded liabilities continue to grow daily. Just as a person making $100,000 and owing over $800,000 is in trouble, so too is our government, for no nation has ever accumulated this much debt. Trillions of dollars are bantered about so often today that it is difficult to conceive their magnitude. Seven trillion one-dollar bills, for example, would stack to the moon (about 250,000 miles away) and back, illustrating that America's debt in dollar bills would go to the moon and back twenty-five times!

The $53 trillion in total American debts, even at just 5% interest, is over $2.65 trillion per year for interest payments. That is more than the total amount collected by the IRS from all Americans in 2019. And the $2.65 trillion in payments isn't paying off the debt; it is simply paying the interest on it. America (and many other nations) is facing a day of reckoning: it must increase taxes, reduce benefits, or default on the national debt. Something, in other words, has to give. In less than fifty years, the total debt has ballooned from *only* $2 trillion to $53 trillion, a twenty-six times increase since the early 1970s!

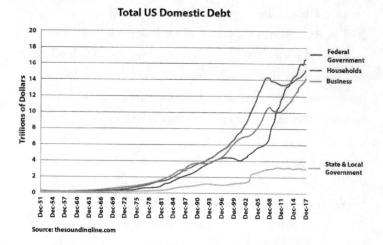

Total US Domestic Debt

Source: thesoundinaline.com

America is bankrupting itself just like the spendthrift who described how he went bankrupt, "Well, slowly at first, but really fast at the end." America is now entering the really fast stage as the monthly total federal budget deficits in 2020 surpass the total federal budget deficits of the first two hundred years!

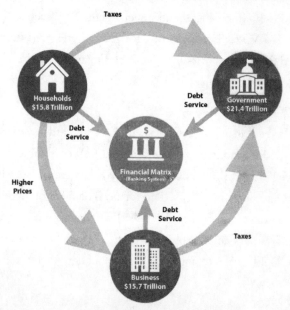

The wealthiest and most productive nation of the twentieth century is about to go bankrupt at the turn of the twenty-first century. How is this possible? What happened to America, the land of the free and the home of the brave? How did it change to the land of indebted serfs and the home of the bankrupt? The short answer is the ever-increasing debts and compound interest overwhelmed the productive capacity of the world's most prosperous nation. Author James Butler observed:

> In 50 short years, debt has gone from being a luxury for a few to a convenience for many to an addiction for most to a disease for all. It is a virus that has spread to every aspect of our economy, from a consumer using a credit card to buy a $0.75 candy bar in a vending machine to a government borrowing trillions to keep the lights on.[3]

The preceding chart points to the underlying problem; namely, debt is siphoning off money from nearly every American household, business, and government. The science fiction movie *The Matrix* is true to life, for human energy is being siphoned from every worker to feed the Financial Matrix.

Household Debts

Between loans, mortgages, and credit cards, Americans are cast adrift rudderless in a sea of debt. According to a 2019 NerdWallet study,[4] American households have more debt today than at any point in history. The financial dangers of debt were aptly demonstrated during the COVID-19 quarantine when millions of American households were debt pinched within two weeks. Debt is like taking a daily shortcut across thin ice. The debtor is confident they will never fall through, even though sooner or later, most do.

American statistics organized by debt category are:

1. Average credit card (CC) revolving debt: $7,104 (59% of CCs have revolving debt)
2. Average mortgage debt: $192,618
3. Average outstanding student loan balance: $46,679
4. Average auto loan debt: $27,934 (many households having multiple car loans)

Combining the average mortgage, car loan, credit card, and student loan debt together, one discovers that the average person is paying interest on approximately $275,000. This results in households paying approximately $1,500 in total compound interest expenses per month. This wealth is siphoned from the borrower to the banks, while the borrower lives paycheck to paycheck, renting the items they think they own. The debt is disastrous in two ways. First, the constant $1,500 siphon on financial resources reduces the opportunities available to advance. Second, debt is like walking on thin ice, and when unforeseen expenses break the ice, the family drowns financially. Consider, for instance, 60% of US bankruptcies are caused by medical-related expenses (medical debts and lost wages), and 28% of these have outstanding balances of over $10,000.

Government Debts

Governments are an expense, and when the government increases its debts, the people must pay the price in either higher taxes or inflation (an increase in the money supply discussed later). Between federal, Social Security, state, and local taxes, approximately half of workers' paychecks are taken by the government, and this is before the effect of inflation and the loss of the dollar's purchasing power are taken into account. Every time the government promises to do something for the people, it must take from the people to do so. Debt, however, allows the government to delay increasing taxes to pay for its commitments and simply borrow the money instead. Needless to say, after decades of kicking the can down the road to avoid the discomfort of raising taxes to pay for political promises, the government is now in a pickle. After all, it now must raise taxes anyway to pay for past promises and debts, but the current taxpayers will not receive any benefit for paying the taxes for past generations' benefits. Author P. J. O'Rourke once said, "Giving money and power to government is like giving whiskey and car keys to teenage boys."[5] Even more dangerous, in reality, is giving government access to practically unlimited amounts of debt over the last fifty years because it predictably resulted in our current debt disaster.

Business Debts

Finally, businesses have fallen in love with borrowing money to fund further investments, instead of the tried-and-true method of reinvesting earnings. This has created a highly unstable business environment where businesses must constantly increase sales merely to service debts, and when they don't, they must borrow even more. Even big businesses that have sales revenue in the billions of dollars annually could not survive two weeks without government cash injections during the COVID-19 quarantine. Nonetheless, business debts are also transferred to the people, who pay higher prices for the products to ensure the businesses can service the $15 trillion in debts.

Business debts and business taxes are simply added to the product price, making consumers fully responsible to pay the bill. Debt is like dancing with the devil. If possible, it's best to skip the dance because once started, the devil calls the tunes and his partner cannot stop until they drop. The people wind up working longer hours for less take-home income to service the compounding business debts. This converts Henry David Thoreau's famous quote about most people leading "lives of quiet desperation" into most people leading 'lives of compounding debt desperation."

Debt Control

Debt-money will be discussed in detail in the next chapter, but it's important to realize it is an illusion, a magician's sleight of hand, created out of thin air and loaned to the people. The people are left with the appearance of freedom, with only the gentlest of prods of monthly payments, barely detectable so long as the debt is paid and the bank profits. Miss a payment, however, and the prod becomes palpable, with houses foreclosed upon, cars repossessed, and credit cards cancelled. The bewildered borrower is subsequently downgraded in credit rating and becomes financially persona non grata. Normally, bankruptcy and harassing calls from debt collectors ensue, seeking to divide any remaining assets. Not surprisingly, the literal meaning of the word mortgage is *death grip*. The borrower, in essence, has slipped a noose around their own neck, and walks back and forth on a plank until the mortgage is paid back, hoping they will never slip and activate the death grip pledge. To summarize, the banks create something out of nothing, loan the nothing to people desiring something, and then the people must earn something to pay back the nothing.

America's Unfunded Government Liabilities

The American government is bankrupting itself. To fund current expenditures, it must borrow money daily. Thus, all unfunded liabilities are huge IOUs because there has been no money saved for the expected expenses. Similar to Ponzi schemes, new loans or tax revenues must come in today to pay yesterday's expenses, or the entire system goes bust. For instance, 90% of existing retirees rely on Social Security as a source of income, with only one in ten able to live comfortably without it. This is why the government's debt is so dangerous to these promised benefits, for even the federal government cannot raise taxes or increase loans indefinitely. At some point, these IOUs will become unpayable, and the Ponzi scheme comes crashing down. Indeed, one of the biggest political issues over the next twenty years will be how to manage expected benefits for retirees while not saddling current workers with incomprehensible tax increases. After all, when Social Security started, the ratio of those who were paying into the system to those collecting was somewhere around forty-two to one. Today the ratio is down to about three to one. It's highly likely this ratio will continue to fall, requiring the government to either decrease proposed benefits or raise taxes even higher, both of which are political dynamite. The unavoidable Social Security issue boils down to this: Is it morally right for the government to tax one generation of taxpayers to pay for the benefits of another? This question remains unanswered and has haunted this much-debated program since its 1935 inception.

For the first $137,700 of personal income, the current Social Security tax is 6.2% for the employer and 6.2% for the employee, or 12.4% total. The current rate for Medicare is 1.45% for the employer and 1.45% for the employee, or 2.9% total.

This is significantly more than the 1935 proposed tax rates that were projected to never rise above 6%. Perhaps the best explanation of the current debt, Social Security, and Medicare crisis comes from author Henry Hazlitt:

> Today is already the tomorrow which the bad economist yesterday urged us to ignore. The long-run consequences of some economic policies may become evident in a few months. Others may not become evident for several years. Still others may not become evident for decades. But in every case those long-run consequences are contained in the policy as surely as the hen was in the egg, the flower in the seed.[6]

Inflation

There is still one more hidden tax the Financial Matrix takes from the people, and this occurs when the money supply is inflated. Inflation degrades the purchasing power (each dollar is worth less) of money between 3–5% annually. This affects society in several ways. First, inflation usually results in higher prices paid by consumers. In 1913, for instance, the year the Federal Reserve central bank was created, four cents had the same purchasing power as a dollar did in 2013, indicating that purchasing power had decreased by a factor of twenty-five in one hundred years! This indicates that the average purchaser needed twenty-five times more money in 2013 than in 1913. Furthermore, the prices appear to be doubling every fifteen years or so, and this silent tax robs the people's wealth while increasing the financial system's profits. Second, inflation helps all governments collect more tax revenues because progressive income tax charges higher rates on higher incomes. Inflation makes it appear incomes are rising, but the increase does not result in real wage growth because each dollar earned is worth less than before. The progressive income tax moves workers into a higher bracket even though their real wage growth is flat. It is estimated that every 1% increase in inflation leads to a $7 billion increase in tax revenues due to the progressive income tax. Therefore, earners are hit with a double whammy, with inflation draining the purchasing power of dollars while falsely inflating incomes and thus forcing higher income taxes. Finally, this tax is particularly brutal for those on fixed incomes because their wages do not adjust upward with inflation. We will discuss inflation and deflation of the money supply further in the coming chapters, but for now it's important to understand that inflation is a tax on the people by the banking system and governments without any vote or accountability.

Inflation and the Business Cycle

In the upcoming chapters we will discuss how the banks create inflation and the subsequent deflation, which cause the boom/bust cycles. As if the inflationary theft of the people's dollars is not bad enough, the banking system has compounded this when the bust cycle causes economic downturns, resulting in job losses, business failures, and bankruptcies. These boom/bust cycles are not once-in-a-lifetime events either. In fact, according to the National Bureau of Economic Research, there have been thirty-three business cycles (boom/bust cycles) between 1854 and 2009, and the full inflationary and deflationary cycle lasted around fifty-six months on average. In other words, the banking system, on top of robbing ninety-six cents of every dollar's purchasing power since 1913, also subjected the people to boom/bust cycles, where the inflation van that ran over the people is reversed to run them over again. To set our economy free from the boom/bust cycle, we must learn its root cause and eliminate it.[7]

Inflation and Flatline Income

The last fifty years changed the trajectory of modern civilization, and it's no coincidence that 1971 (nearly fifty years ago) was also the year the global banking system gained absolute control over the world's money supply. Predictably, right after the Financial Matrix gained control, inflation exploded, and the people's pay raises imploded. In fact, according to the Pew Research graphic below, pay raises ended completely, with people producing more while all the gains were siphoned into the financial system. Pre-1971, the workers did receive real wage growth just as free market theory would predict, but post-1971 is another story completely.

Predictably, right after the birth of the global Financial Matrix in 1971 and its subsequent control of the money supply, inflation exploded, real wages stagnated, and boom/bust cycles became a worldwide phenomenon of greater magnitude than ever before. The graphic shows how the Financial Matrix is destroying the middle class, the backbone of any free society. According to the Social Security Administration, the median American annual wage was just $34,248.45 in 2019. In other words, half of all American workers made less than $2,854.05

per month, placing them just above the poverty line. Further-more, since 1950 the Financial Matrix has gutted home equity percentages (the amount of value remaining after subtracting all mortgage debts) from over 80% in the early 1950s to barely 30% today.

This is nearly a 50% reduction in home equities from Amer-ica's $25 trillion housing market, indicating that $12.5 trillion in value has been siphoned from American society and into the Financial Matrix in less than seventy years. In other words, the middle class is maintaining appearances only by mortgaging the generational wealth willed to them, including their homes. This cannot go on indefinitely. The damage done by the Financial Matrix is coming into view, as the unprecedented levels of per-sonal, business, and government debts must ultimately be paid from the people's production, turning the financial dreams of billions of people into nightmares.[8]

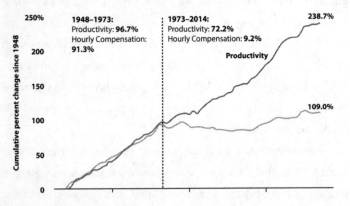

Note: Data are for average hourly compensation of production/nonsupervisory workers in the private sector and net productivity of the total economy. "Net Productivity" is the growth of output of goods and services minus depreciation per hour worked.

Source: Pew Research Center

Thankfully, the world doesn't end when a nation defaults on its debts, but it does communicate the need for meaning-ful change. Since the Renaissance, the financial system has been littered with economic growth-and-collapse scenarios because the banking system has been unable to provide a stable money supply. As a result, many nations rose to greatness, overindebted themselves to maintain it, and then collapsed when the compound interest overran its ability to service the debts. When history routinely repeats itself, one should take notice of the underlying system at work. It now appears that America is about to experience these painful systemic lessons. However, the important thing is to learn from the experience; as George Santayana said, "Those who cannot remember the past are condemned to repeat it."[9] In fact, this book will reveal how and why the defective financial system causes the world economy to toggle between growth and collapse cycles. The goal, however, is not just to expose the defects of the current financial system, but also to propose the systemic resolution to end five hundred years of financial instability. The dream is to restore financial justice for all by creating a fair and equitable financial system and end the Financial Matrix. To do so, however, we must first understand compound interest and why it is so crushing to the modern economy.

The Wonders of Compound Interest

Few people comprehend how destructive trillions of dollars of compounding debt interest is to people, businesses, and nations. Albert Einstein, however, was one who did, and after studying the intricacies of compounding interest, he allegedly proclaimed: "Compound interest is the eighth wonder of the world. He who understands it, earns it . . . he who doesn't pays it."[10] The $53 trillion in total American debt reveals that time is not on America's side, which is why debt should be treated like cancer and removed. For instance, imagine a young man

working in the manger during the birth of Jesus. He saw the
three wise men give gifts and wanted to give also, but he had
only his penny-equivalent wage. Embarrassed to give such a
small amount, he instead deposited the penny into a no-fees
investment account at 5% annual interest and gave it to Joseph.
Generation after generation, this money compounded with no
further money deposited, until, as the closest surviving relative,
you received the *penny* gift. How much is your *small* investment
worth by the year 2015? Before guessing, let me encourage you
to guess much higher, as the total is astronomical. In fact, the
total is in excess of 47 million Earth-sized spheres of pure gold!
Of course, there isn't this much gold, so this is impossible, but
the math is correct. This extreme example indicates that compound interest loses touch with reality after extended periods of
time. This is one of the primary reasons why compound debt
interest should be treated like the plague—avoided at all costs.

   Let's do the math on $0.01 invested at 5% compound inter-
est rate per year:

Years	Amount in Dollars
15	0.02 (It took about fifteen years for the penny to double.)
30	0.04
70	0.30
150	15.07
200	172.92
250	1,983
378	1,022,245 (In 378 years, the savings account has over one million dollars.)
500	Over 393 million

These dollar amounts are getting so big, let's convert the totals into tons of gold (1,000 kilograms per metric ton), setting the price of gold at $60,000 per kilogram:

500	6.6 tons of gold
600	862 tons
800	14,903,491 tons
1,000	257,719,820,121 tons
1,200	4,456,640,817,128,200 tons
1,400	77,066,821,494,330,600,000 tons
1,490	The gold is now heavier than the Earth. (The Earth weighs 6 billion trillion metric tons.)
1,525	This is a gold sphere the size of the Earth and 5.5 times heavier than the Earth.
1,800	698,350 gold spheres the size of Earth (The actual global supply of gold only fills a little more than three Olympic-sized swimming pools.)
2,000	12,076,273,761 gold spheres the size of Earth
2,020	32,041,949,559 gold spheres the size of Earth

The 2020 total dollar value of the original penny investment is now $63,443,059,922,674,400,000,000,000,000,000,000,000, which is over $63,443 trillion trillion trillion. This makes the actual total worldwide money ($83.6 trillion) seem hardly more than spitting in the penny-compounded ocean. As such, compound interest is no laughing matter. In fact, divide this amount by the total population on Earth (around 7.8 billion), and every person alive would be millions of times wealthier than the wealthiest person alive; everyone would have a beach worth of money compared to Jeff Bezos holding only a grain of sand. How is this possible? A society's wealth is created from human production, not compounding numbers; however, debt pits the physically limited productive world against the metaphysically unlimited mathematical world. Over time, the unlimited mathematical debt interest will always outrun the limited physical human production. No wonder the Biblical Jubilee resets compound interest every forty-nine years, knowing compound interest over longer periods of time becomes disconnected from reality. To be sure, thousands of years of compound interest is extreme; however, the truth is the banking system has been compounding interest (loaning trillions, not just one penny) for almost four thousand years (not just 2,015 years). Furthermore, the banks loaned it to billions of people, not just one, and charged significantly higher than 5% interest most of the time. Altogether, the amount paid into the banking system from the people's production is inconceivable, and when global monopoly profits and power are the reward for indebting the people, it's highly unlikely the Financial Matrix will want to change.

How Debt Kills Dreams

A recent Wells Fargo study disclosed that millennials and Gen Z needed half of their total income to pay debts, and a University of Arizona study revealed that half of college graduates still needed financial help from family members two years after completing school.[12] Increasing debt, dismally, has caused millennials to be the first American generation that will not enjoy a higher quality of life than their parents. No wonder these students still need family support. This is because they have tens of thousands of dollars of debt before adding on room, board, and transportation expenses. A famous maxim says the lesson is continued until the lesson is learned, and in the case of the dangers of debt, few seem to be learning the lesson—namely, that debt smothers dreams. Indeed, until the people learn the priceless dangers of debt, Winston Churchill's famous statement, "Never in the field of human conflict was so much owed by so many to so few," must now read, "Never in the field of human economy has so much been owed by so many to so few." America was once the envy of the free world, known for its liberty and justice for all. Now it's known for its debt. Indeed, the only group advancing in America today is the elites, not the 1%, but the .01%, those who have connections to tap into the money created out of thin air. The following chart is broken up into quintiles (five equal portions of 20% each) of the total population because inflation and debts compound equally regardless of a person's wealth. Thus, the people on the lower income scales suffer far greater consequences from out-of-control debts and inflation, with the income siphoned off being the difference between surviving financially and falling through the

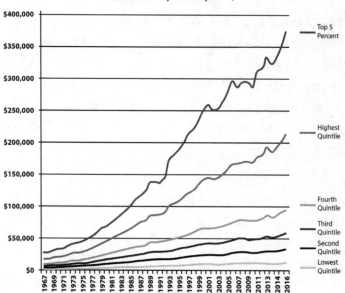

Average U.S. Household Income 1967–2016
(Quintiles plus Top 5%)

thin ice. This chart reveals the Financial Matrix injustices in all their infamy and why financial justice is so badly needed.

Debt Stress

One final consequence of debt to consider is the massive increase in stress levels from no longer feeling in control of one's financial future. Whereas the financial ramifications are obvious enough, when the physical and emotional toll is added, the full debt picture comes into view. I remember how helpless Laurie and I felt, that no matter what we did, we were no longer the captains of our financial ship—as if we had invited the debt pirate on board and before we knew it, he had led a successful mutiny with his menacing compounding friends. Now we were forced to either obey his monthly dictates or walk the financial plank. Indeed, in 2014, the American Psychological Association (APA) studied more than 3,000 American adults; 72% admitted feeling stressed about money during the previous month, and 26% said they felt financially stressed most or all the time. Strikingly, 54% admitted they had *just enough* or *not enough* money to meet monthly needs.[13] Debts too high and incomes too low are the vice squeezing joy out of the people, changing the familiar saying "No pain, no gain" to the banking system's "Your pain is our gain."

Gold is the money of kings, silver is the money of gentlemen, barter is the money of peasants—but debt is the money of slaves.

—Norm Franz

CHAPTER 2

Money and Fractional
Reserve Banking

What Is Money?

Although most people work more than ninety thousand hours in a lifetime to earn money, less than one in a thousand can properly define what money is. Sure, they know how to make money, spend money, and borrow money, but ironically, they toil forty years for an undefined entity. Needless to say, the Financial Matrix has reaped a bountiful harvest on this account. Thankfully, however, in less than four hours (the time it takes to read this book) you can start your journey to financial literacy. This is the subject you should have learned in school, providing the keys to escaping the Financial Matrix.

Financial literacy begins with an understanding of money: what it is, how it was created, and how the Financial Matrix has captured it. Money, in itself, is not bad. In fact, it's one of the greatest economic innovations in recorded history, and a vital aspect of a free market economy (to be discussed further in a later chapter). Before money, trade could be difficult because barter required both parties to desire the other's goods and services, what economists call a double coincidence of wants. If only one party wanted what the other had to offer, then the swap would be difficult, unless they could find a third party who wanted what they offered and had items both of them desired.

Eventually, people realized certain items seemed to be accepted by nearly all parties because they were desired by nearly everyone within society. Once this was realized, bartering was easy because it used the most marketable commodity to complete most transactions. Money, in other words, is the most marketable commodity used as the medium of exchange. And with money, the bartering of goods and services exploded because practically everyone accepted it, knowing they could then barter money in exchange for other goods and services. Historically, humans have used many different items for money, including beads, seashells, feathers, big rocks, tobacco, cattle, salt, and precious metal coins. Money increased trade, trade increased wealth, and wealth increased the demand for even more goods and services. Money became the tool to ensure any excess production was easy to exchange in the market economy. Noncoercive exchanges are always win-win because if both parties are not satisfied, the transaction will not occur, making free trade either win-win or no deal.

Supply   **Demand**

Precious Metal Money

Medium of Exchange

After experimenting with various forms of money, precious metals became the preferred money of ancient civilizations. In fact, the first precious metal coins were stamped in Lydia, and from there gold and silver coins spread throughout ancient civilization, including Greece and Rome. However, after the fall of the Roman Empire in the fifth century AD, precious metal coins fell into disuse during the European Middle Ages. Nonetheless, in the fifteenth century, during the Italian Renaissance, precious metal coins experienced a rebirth. This led to an explosion in production and commerce as wealth began to spread throughout Europe. Money revived European monarchs who were exposed to the Byzantine money system during the Crusades. Western Europe gradually freed itself from the feudal-era land monopoly, as the serfs matriculated into the cities, began producing goods and services, and used money to trade goods and services with one another.

Because money is the most marketable commodity within society and Western Europeans favored precious metals, particularly gold and silver, they became the preferred money source. After all, precious metals met the three essential qualities of legitimate money: 1) a convenient medium of exchange, 2) a consistent measure of value, and 3) a safe store of value because they were durable, portable, divisible, uniform, scarce, acceptable, and had a stable supply. Since precious metals are a commodity, an asset with a fairly limited quantity on Earth (they cannot be created out of thin air), they have been in demand as a store of value since the beginning of recorded history. Money isn't just any asset, however; it is the most marketable one, meaning it can be traded quickly for any other item in the marketplace. Precious metals became the money source during the Renaissance because nearly everyone would accept them to complete any transaction.

Expansion of the Money Supply

Unfortunately, with money comes power, and as wealth expanded, so too did the power of the European monarchs. The more power they gained, the more they wanted, which led the European monarchs to seek power by immoral methods such as what the Roman Caesars practiced in the later Roman Empire: the debasement of the precious metal coins. Debasement is the expansion of the money supply (the total supply of coins) by reducing the precious metal content in each coin. The Caesars would collect the coins in the realm, melt them down, and add base metal mixtures to reduce the precious metal content per coin.

The result increased the number of coins reminted because of the addition of base metals, which increased the total money supply by the increase in total coins. Debasement, in other words, was an inflation (an artificial increase) of the total money supply through decreasing the precious metal content, and hence the asset value of each coin. For example, the graphic below shows that one denarius coin at 95% silver (the percentage of silver content when the denarius was first minted) had the same weight of silver as 190 coins did at 0.5% silver (the percentage of silver content of the last denarius coins minted). Inflation, in other words, had increased the money supply of denarius coins by 19,000% in just over three centuries!

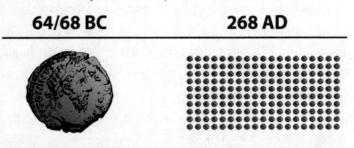

64/68 BC   268 AD

1 Coin at 95% Silver ═ 190 Coins at 0.5% Silver

The Caesars, in effect, were able to rob the people's wealth without having to go through the inconvenient step of raising taxes and used the new money to solidify their power. Debasement became the common practice of each new Caesar. He would collect the coins of the realm, ostensibly to place his image on the reminted coins, but in reality to create more coins (inflation is an artificial expansion of the money supply, which is why adding base metals to the precious metal coins is the earliest form of inflation) for the Caesars to spend through debasing the precious metal content of the coins even further.

Silver Content of a Roman Denarius

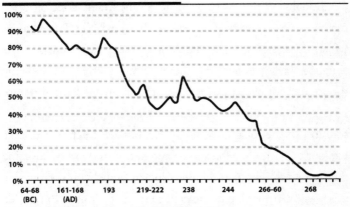

Source: http://www.tulane.edu/-august/handouts.601cprin.htm

This robbed the people of a portion of their assets because the precious metal was the asset and there was less of it in each coin after debasement. Accordingly, the coins, although still a convenient medium of exchange, failed to meet the final two qualities of money because the routine debasements of the Roman coins made them no longer a consistent measure of value nor a store of value.

Interestingly, there were several factors in place protecting society from the greed of the government and its use of overly aggressive inflations of the money supply. First, they could not hide their debasement of the precious metal coins. Second, because the debasement of money was a very labor-intensive process (unlike today's money printing and digitized debts), it slowed the rate of inflation. Nonetheless, once debasement is begun, it always ends in the complete destruction of money. For example, the Roman denarius, the main coin of the Roman Empire, started at over 90% purity of silver content, but was debased to under 1%, destroying its monetary value. The collapse of Roman money led to the collapse of the Roman economy, and as much as anything else, this led to the collapse of the Roman Empire.

Roughly a thousand years later, the fragmented governments (cities, monarchies, and duchies) of the Renaissance, which competed against one another for power and prestige, sought a faster, easier, and more private method of inflating the money supply to increase power but at the same time not raise the ire of the people. The Renaissance banks proposed a solution to the local governments' dilemma: fractional reserve banking (FRB), a much simpler and secret method of inflating the money supply than the debasing of actual coins. However, this was only possible if the governments promised to provide legal cover for the banks to get away with it. Thus was born the partnership between government and banks, the essential core ingredient of today's Financial Matrix.

The History of Fractional Reserve Banking

The FRB fraud was developed by Renaissance goldsmiths, although some claim it was practiced in ancient Babylon. The goldsmiths offered to safely store precious metal, providing a paper gold certificate, a metaphysical representation (similar to a property title) of a physical quantity of gold. Not surprisingly, the paper certificates were discovered to be safer and easier than carrying gold coins that could now just be stored with the goldsmith. Thus, in many instances, the paper certificates became the preferred medium of exchange instead of physical gold coins. Moreover, the new recipient of the certificate in a transaction did not need to reclaim the gold because they could simply reuse the certificate in their next transaction.

The goldsmiths soon noticed most of the gold stored in their vaults remained unclaimed. Unfortunately, the temptation to profit from this *idle* gold was too great. The goldsmiths started creating more gold certificates than actual physical gold stored in their vaults, and even though they produced five to ten times more certificates than gold, they were confident the fraud was undetectable, since most people merely reused the gold certificates, never reclaiming the gold.

Not surprisingly, in every field where metaphysical titles represent physical items, the law protects against fraud through title searches. This ensures the buyer is the sole owner of the title and the physical property. Curiously, however, this was not the case with gold certificates and gold. The bankers, in other words, received a special treatment because they had partnered with Renaissance governments to inflate the money supply. What is illegal in any other field (selling multiple metaphysical titles to the same physical property) was legalized in the field of banking. The disgraceful partnership between banks and governments converted inflation from a time-consuming public action that risked society's displeasure, as in ancient Rome, into the simple and secretive FRB process of printing unbacked precious metal certificates. This fractional reserve banking system quickly became the accepted banking practice throughout the world.

Fractional Reserve Biking

Since FRB is practiced universally, few realize how outrageous it actually is. Perhaps the fraudulent nature of fractional reserve practices would become clearer if we envisioned their use in another field.

Imagine a clever man who owns a repair shop and restores motorcycles for a living. He placed one of his restored bikes up for sale and received an interesting proposal. The buyer promised to pay full price if he could store the bike at the seller's repair shop because he did not have a garage himself. Furthermore, the buyer, respectful of the seller's time, promised to use the motorcycle on Saturdays only, since it was his day off. The seller couldn't believe his luck; even though he sold the bike for full price, it was still in his garage every day but Saturday. In fact, he took the bike out himself for joyrides during the week without the owner's knowledge or permission. Further, he reasoned the bike wasn't doing anyone any good just sitting there. This led to his breakthrough idea. Wouldn't society be better served if the bike was used to full capacity? Enter the concept of *Fractional Reserve Biking*, in which the seller could sell the same bike to multiple buyers. Of course, he would be selling only the metaphysical title to the bike, and so he just needed to find other buyers who agreed to store the bike at his garage. After all, the key to the fractional reserve sleight of hand is separating the physical entity from its metaphysical representation.

In short order, the seller found six more buyers, created six more motorcycle titles, and proceeded to sell the counterfeit titles to six more *owners*. The seller arranged a specific day of the week for each owner to ride the bike, and the sales were finalized. The seller, as a result, successfully sold the same bike seven times, creating an impossible situation where seven people believe they own 100% of a physical bike, even though there is only one. Unlike fractional reserve ownership—where each owner purchases 1/7 share of the single bike, balancing the bike's title among seven owners, which is perfectly legal—fractional reserve biking sells 7/7 of a bike to seven separate people, which is perfectly illegal because it is a physical impossibility.

Although the motorcycle FRB example may seem silly, it is essentially what banks do with our money every single day. This concept is so misunderstood that many otherwise smart people look on it in wonder, as though this invisible fraud were a good thing!

Author Jack Weatherford waxed eloquently in praise of FRB, stating how a Renaissance noble's one hundred gold florins that used to sit idle now mysteriously benefited multiple parties:

> Even though only one hundred gold coins were involved, the miracle of banking deposits and loans had transformed them into many hundreds of florins that could be used by different individuals in different cities at the same time. This new banking money opened vast new commercial avenues for merchants, manufacturers, and investors. Everyone had more money: it was sheer magic.[1]

When monetary historians explain FRB with terms like "magic," "mystery," and "alchemy," one has to wonder if they do not understand how it works or are being purposefully disingenuous. After all, economic science is rational, logical, and systematic. Therefore, although magic may be one possible answer as to how numerous buyers hold identical titles to the same physical piece of gold at the same time, fraud is the more logical explanation.

Indeed, real estate companies request title searches to protect buyers from fraudulent sellers. Strangely, however, no one has thought to do similarly with the vital fields of banking and money. The FRB fraud would be exposed if the same ethical standards were applied to banking as to other forms of titled property. I wonder if Weatherford would defend our wayward motorcycle seller in a court of law by invoking *magic* as a legitimate defense? Would he claim, "Even though only one motorcycle was involved, the miracle of the garage storage and extra paper titles transformed the bike into numerous bikes, each owned by different people, in different locations, all at the same time. The new selling method opened vast new avenues of profit. Everyone had more motorcycles: it was sheer magic."? I believe Weatherford would be laughed out of the courtroom.

There are only two conclusions possible then, when reading these types of comments by otherwise intelligent economists and historians: 1) they didn't dig deep enough to realize that FRB wasn't magic but rather a fraud, or 2) they understood very clearly what it was and were complicit in helping to cover it up with nebulous terms such as magic.

This, in fact, once happened in a courtroom, when Lawrence V. Morgan, the acting president of the First National Bank of Montgomery, testified about the banking system in the 1968 Credit River Case. Normally, the banking system limits exposure to its practices in courtrooms, with most cases being quashed before trial. Nonetheless, when a case does go to trial, the bank president usually gives routine testimony about the specific mortgage to prove the defendant signed the papers and receives a positive ruling. In this case, however, under cross examination, the trial lawyer Jerome Daly asked the banker, "If you were just opening up your bank and no one had yet made a deposit, and I came into your bank and wanted to take out a loan of $18,000, could you loan me that money?" When Morgan said, "Yes," Daly then asked, "Does this mean that you can create money out of thin air?" And the bank president said, "Yes, we can create money out of thin air." Imagine the scene for a moment. Under oath, the president admitted his bank created the money for the loan credit by mere annotations in its books for the note and mortgage of May 8, 1964. The credit, in other words, came into existence out of thin air when the bank created it. Morgan also freely admitted that he knew of no US law that gave the bank permission to do this, commenting it was just standard bank practice.

Clearly, this supported the defense's argument, that there was no lawful consideration for the note because the bank had parted with absolutely nothing of value to create the money, other than a piece of paper with some ink on it. At this point, residing Justice Martin V. Mahoney publicly stated, "It sounds like fraud to me," and everybody in the courtroom nodded in agreement. The jury ruled unanimously for the defendant, but not surprisingly, the case was thrown out on appeal because the bank alleged Mahoney had no jurisdiction to rule on the banking issue, even though the bank had agreed to Mahoney's jurisdiction originally. Evidently, the banks agree to jurisdiction only under favorable rulings. Interestingly, the bankers did not complain that they did not receive a fair trial and, to President Morgan's enduring credit, he had told truths that, although more widely known today, were shocking revelations in 1968.[2]

The FRB system is fraud because the same piece of precious metal cannot physically be given to ten different parties simultaneously, but the monetary powers realized ten metaphysical titles could be. What was physically impossible became metaphysically possible, unbelievably profitable, and extremely difficult to detect. The FRB system creates money out of thin air and then loans it to people, businesses, and governments, who must work to pay back the principal and interest. In other words, the banks create something out of nothing, loan the nothing to societies wanting something, and the people then earn something to pay back the nothing. Murray Rothbard, the late dean of the Austrian School of Economics, minced no words when describing the FRB fraud: "It should be clear that modern fractional reserve banking (FRB) is a shell game, a Ponzi scheme, a fraud in which fake warehouse receipts are issued and circulate as equivalent to the cash supposedly represented by those receipts."[3]

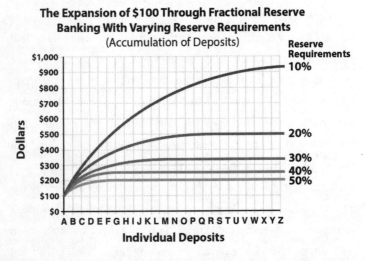

Note: Reserve requirement means how much the government requires banks to actually have on deposit physically compared to how much they can loan out.

From a big-picture perspective, the practice of FRB expands the overall money supply, a result that has huge ramifications for the economy and individuals. It's important to look at how this takes place. A Renaissance bank with 10% reserves could theoretically expand 100 pounds of gold into 1,000 pounds of loans, since the 100 pounds is a 10% reserve of 1,000 pounds of gold loans. The FRB system, in this event, has created 900 pounds of gold credit out of thin air. The following chart depicts just how much the money supply can expand when doing the exact same thing the Renaissance banks did, only on a larger scale.

Linear Versus Systems Thinking

The fraudulent creation of money titles is the major issue with the FRB system, but this leads to a secondary issue just as damaging, and that is the inherent instability of the debt-money supply created by it. To understand why the FRB system is inherently unstable, however, we must learn the difference between holistic systems thinking and linear cause-and-effect thinking.[4] Whereas we are trained to think linearly with a cause-and-effect mindset where A leads to B and results in C, in systems theory, sometimes C can cause A or a combination of A and C can result in B because the world is often messier than simple linear situations. Systems thinking, in other words, is not linear, for it does not happen in a straight line. Instead, it occurs in loops because each part of the system is interdependent, meaning an event in one part of the loop creates a wave that affects every other part. This is called the feedback loop, and every system is a system because it has a feedback loop. Although this sounds more complicated than the simple linear thinking we are usually taught, it is much more representative of reality and therefore a better map for the territory.

Therefore, when linear thinking is applied to systemic problems, the feedback loop is ignored. The result is wrong conclusions and nonsense. Perhaps an illustration will show this more clearly. Imagine a rug merchant who noticed a bump under one of his rugs. He stepped on the bump to flatten it out, but the bump, like a wave in water, merely reappeared in another spot. The man repeatedly stepped on the bump and watched it reappear elsewhere. Finally, an angry snake slithered out from under the rug. The merchant's linear solution (remove the bump by stepping on it) was ineffective because he was actually dealing with a system. The rug, bump, snake, and the man's foot all interacted to cause the snake to respond to an ongoing feedback loop. The man's step on the bump caused the snake to move to a safe spot, which of course produced a new bump, and a new feedback loop began. Fortunately, the aggravated snake (the underlying problem) removed itself from the system, but this is rarely the case in real life, where the failed linear interventions only make the underlying problem worse.

Interestingly, although systems are everywhere, there are only two main types of feedback loops. The first is reinforcing loops, where a change in the system serves as a signal for further change in the same direction. Reinforcing loops cause either runaway (1) exponential growth or (2) exponential decline, depending on whether they are positive or negative reinforcing loops. The other main feedback loop is balancing feedback, where a change in the system serves as a signal for change in the opposite direction as the goal-seeking system seeks to restore the lost balance. The balanced feedback, in other words, is goal seeking, striving to maintain equilibrium by recalibrating toward a certain value or situation.

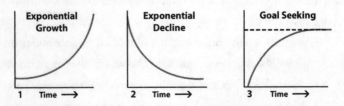

The world's economic system is a balanced feedback system loop whose components are constantly updating to balance the money supply with the supply and demand for every good and service within the marketplace. Thus, we must study the economy systematically because it has balanced feedback loops, and any intervention in one part of the economy interacts with every other part like a wave in a pool.

I share this architecture so people can see how the FRB system is a fraudulent intervention into the balanced economy. The artificial expansion of the money supply manipulates price signals, temporarily imbalancing the system, until the economic factors (price, supply, and demand) adjust to restore dynamic equilibrium at the new money-supply level.

FRB's intervention into the balanced economy system is similar to a binge drinker's alcoholic intervention into the balanced bodily system because both temporarily imbalance a naturally balanced system. The binge drinker's amusing slogan, "One beer is too many and a million is not enough," explains the systemic effect of alcohol intervention on the human body. It also illustrates the artificial debt-money intervention because any expansion of the money supply is too many and a million is not enough. The positive reinforcing cycles (beer leads to more beer and debt-money leads to more debt-money) continue until the balanced system can handle no more. Because balanced systems must recalibrate, the positive reinforcement loop cannot last forever and eventually must reverse to rebalance the system. When it reverses, the positive reinforcing loop transforms into a negative reinforcing loop because the overconsumption of beer and debt leads to the balanced systems counteracting it with sickness and sleep for too much beer and insolvency defaults for too much debt. In consequence, every intervention into the body or economy creates an artificial boom followed by a real bust as the system rebalances.

INFLATION
Prices Increase with the Money Supply

Supply   **Demand**

Limited   Unlimited

Money Supply
Increases

1. FRB loans lead to further FRB loans.
2. This positive reinforcing loop expands Money Supply
3. Inflation is an expansion of the Money Supply

Fractional Reserve Banking Is the Cause of the Boom/Bust Business Cycle

This is why the FRB systemic inflation is even more cata-
strophic than debasement. Whereas the debasement of coins
merely expands the money supply by increasing the total number of coins, the FRB system inflation increases and decreases
the money supply (through the positive and negative reinforcing
loops). This introduces a new phenomenon—deflation, a decrease of the money supply—into the monetary equation. As if
increasing the money supply (inflation) wasn't bad enough (like
getting run over by a van), the FRB system, unlike debasement,
can also decrease the money supply (deflation) when loans are
paid off or defaulted on (as if the van subsequently reverses and
runs over us again). The Roman debasement was inflationary
theft because it increased the money supply by the additional
coinage mixed with base metals. Nonetheless, it did not have
a deflation component (the decrease of the money supply) because the additional coins were a physical reality, not created
out of thin air, and therefore, they could not vanish into thin
air. In contrast, in the FRB system, debt-money is created out

of thin air (causing inflation) and vanishes into thin air (causing deflation), which occurs with every loan opened and closed. Therefore, the boom/bust cycle that has plagued the modern economy is a direct result of the systemic inflation/deflation oscillation inherent within the FRB system.

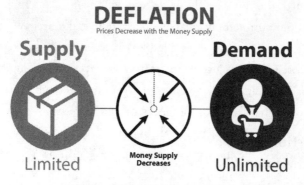

DEFLATION
Prices Decrease with the Money Supply

Supply

Demand

Limited

**Money Supply
Decreases**

Unlimited

1. Without new FRB loans, defaults begin on older FRB loans.
2. This negative reinforcing loop decreases Money Supply
3. Deflation is a contraction of the Money Supply.

The inherent oscillation within the FRB system is one of its defects; the other is its mathematical absurdity because total debts increase faster than the total money supply, which makes it an inherently unsustainable system. FRB loans must be procured this month (increasing the money supply) in order to pay the debts accrued in past months. And if new FRB debt-money is not created, the old debts become unpayable, and the wave of defaults begins. In other words, the boom expansion of the FRB debt-money loans (the positive reinforcing loop inflation) continues until the banks cannot loan any more money (from either the banks or the people reaching loan limits). Then, because there is not enough debt-money in existence to service all the loans, the bust contraction of the FRB debt-money begins (the negative reinforcing loop deflation) with the least solvent borrowers defaulting first. Once deflation begins, round after round of defaults occur, crashing the money supply (deflation) and exposing the FRB systems' inherent lack of reserves.

The problem with FRB loans is debt-money must continue to expand (positive reinforcing loops) until the banks can no longer loan any more money. And as soon as this point is reached, the most insolvent debtors will begin defaulting, crescendoing throughout the banking system as the money supply seeks to return to its original level. Booms lead to bust (negative reinforcing loops) just as predictably as throwing balls up leads to balls coming back down. Moreover, even though the money supply has deflated, the prices of products and services are still inflated. The FRB system boom has caused an unnatural inflation of the money supply and prices, and now the bust is a period of deflation of the money supply and prices back to pre-inflation levels. Recessions and depressions are periods of stagnation caused by the supply of goods still being priced at the inflated money-supply levels while the money supply has been deflated to a lower money-supply level. The duration of the recession/depression stagnations depends on the time it takes for the market to recalibrate prices and wages to the now-deflated money supply. The mathematical imbalance between total debt-money and total debts is inherent within the FRB system. This is what causes the boom-cycle inflation and the bust-cycle deflation. As a result, the only way to end the boom/bust cycle is to end the FRB system that caused it.

To elaborate, consider the following example: If a person obtains a $250,000 mortgage at 5% interest for thirty years, the FRB system creates $250,000 of new debt-money, but no money is created to pay the interest on the debt. Thus, the borrower owes $250,000 in principal, plus another $233,000 in interest over the duration of the loan (a total of $488,000), even though only $250,000 of total money was created. The only way the borrower can raise the additional funds to pay the mortgage is to compete with other borrowers for the limited money supply when compared to the total debts. There is simply not enough money available to pay off all the debts. This is the systematic defect of the FRB fraud, that the interest owed was never created, so how, exactly, can something be paid back to the lender that does not exist? Moreover, with every additional FRB loan, the total debts increase faster than the total money supply.

FRB is nothing more than a game of musical chairs where every loan expands the gap between the total money supply and the total debts. And the only way to keep the music going is to continually expand the number of FRB loans. Since there are more dollars owed than created, if the music ever stops and all the money is demanded, we would discover there is not enough to pay back what is owed (because it was never created), and the economy would come crashing down. The game of musical chairs forces society to borrow from Peter to pay Paul until the unsustainable model leads to another global economic meltdown, as in 2008 and 2020.

The following chart illustrates the inherent problem: the US money supply is around $15 trillion, but total debts are over $50 trillion. It is impossible for $15 trillion to pay back $50 trillion, which indicates that the only way this can continue is for more debt-money to be created. This is a monetary game of musical chairs. There is no way every government, business, and person can pay off all of their debts because of the FRB system's imbalance between the total debt-money supply and the total debts. If all bank loans were demanded to be paid back today, over two-thirds of the debts could not be paid and the world would discover it is completely insolvent due to the fractional reserve banking system. This fraudulent system has created an unnatural scarcity in the money supply compared to total debts and the game of musical chairs can only continue as long as more money can be borrowed from the Financial Matrix. When no more FRB loans are forthcoming, the music stops and the boom turns to bust.

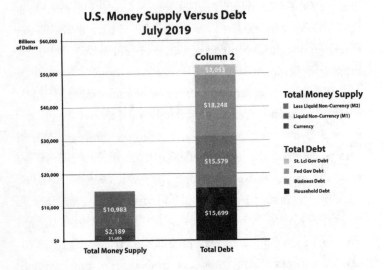

The FRB system can rise and fall, but because of its very architecture, it can never stabilize. The FRB system is wreaking havoc on the global economy because it is wholly incapable of providing the one thing the free market money system needs—namely, stability. A stable money supply is foundational for the free market (discussed further in Chapter 5) because it provides entrepreneurs with accurate, non-manipulated price signals, which end the dreaded boom/bust cycles and increase the wealth for everyone. From the people's perspective, it is sheer lunacy to build the world's money supply upon the most unstable of moneys: FRB debt-money. However, from the banking elites' perspective, it is sheer genius because they have achieved absolute power and profits.

This inherent instability we've just discussed is dangerous not only to the economy and individuals, but also to the fractional reserve banks. That is, the FRB system must collapse because it is systemically insolvent. Therefore, the fractional reserve banks have, throughout history, sought to centralize their fractional reserves as historian Gabriel Kolko noted: "The entire banking movement, at all crucial stages, was centralized in the hands of a few men who for years were linked, ideologically and personally, with one another."[5] The banks combined to protect against potential defaults when the proverbial music stopped. The goal was to mitigate the downside risk of a total FRB collapse while enjoying the upside rewards of FRB profits. Today's global centralized Financial Matrix is a direct result of the inherent instability of the FRB fraud that drove the participating banks to join forces. In the next chapter, we will see how the financial elites created a worldwide partnership (today's Financial Matrix) to protect the FRB system—the goose that lays the golden eggs.

It is well enough that people of the nation do not understand our banking and monetary system, for if they did, I believe there would be a revolution before tomorrow morning.

—Henry Ford

CHAPTER 3

Central Banks, Gold Standard, and the Financial Matrix

The FRB system is a banking cartel (a group of independent banks working in tandem to achieve monopoly-like profits and stability) who believed that if they pooled the limited fractional reserves of each individual bank, the combined reserves would reduce the inherent instability. The FRB system, however, no matter how many fractional reserve banks join together, will never achieve balance because, as noted in the last chapter, it is a game of musical chairs that is systemically imbalanced and therefore not predictable. Unless protected by the nation-state or a central bank supported by the nation-state, the FRB system is a walking time bomb; the bank cartel thrives when the music is playing (during the boom) and collapses when the music stops (during the bust). Governments, in consequence, were forced to rescue the banking system, either by providing funds or by temporarily removing the gold redeemability of the paper money until the bust period was over. For instance, Murray Rothbard explained how the FRB system was protected by the American government that allowed the banks to suspend the convertibility of paper money (an admission that they were insolvent and unable to return the customers' precious metal money) into precious metals upon customer demand:

Specie (gold or silver) payments were suspended from August 1814 to February 1817. For two and a half years could banks expand while issuing what was in effect fiat paper and bank deposits. From then on, every time there was a banking crisis brought on by inflationary expansion and demands for redemption in specie, state and federal governments looked the other way and permitted general suspension of specie payments while bank operations continued to flourish. It became clear to the banks that in a general crisis they would not be required to meet the ordinary obligations of contract law or of respect for property rights, so their inflationary expansion was permanently encouraged by this massive failure of government to fulfill its obligation to enforce contracts and defend the rights of property.[1]

This instability was caused by the inherent imbalance between the total money supply and total FRB debts, and cannot be fixed by combining any number of imbalanced musical-chair games together. After all, just as combining "X" number of imbalanced musical-chair games does not create a balanced game, neither does combining "X" number of imbalanced fractional reserve banks achieve a balanced system. Each individual bank is an unstable system; therefore, combining a bunch of unstable banks (mini-systems) into one bigger system cannot magically produce stability. Thus, once the first bank is bailed out, the fractional reserves are quickly depleted, leaving the entire system further exposed when the next bank collapses into insolvency. The FRB cartel was wholly unable to protect itself from bank failures due to the inherently imbalanced nature of the FRB system.

FRB Central Banks

Faced with this problem that threatened their very profitable game, FRB participants realized they needed a more powerful backstop than merely combining their limited reserves together.

Thus, in an effort to unite the fractional banks even closer while hoping to stabilize the highly imbalanced system, the FRB cartel proposed another intervention to the supportive national governments. This one would further centralize the money supply by creating a central bank, a bank for bankers, to protect the FRB systems from insolvency during the bust period by becoming the lender of last resort. Any time the FRB system was endangered by its inherent lack of reserves, the thought was the central bank could create money and inject it into the banks to protect them from collapse. The Bank of England (BoE) was the first fully functional central bank, and it was supported by the English monarchs, who were able to borrow money cheaply from the BoE without having to haggle with parliament. Of course, other European governments followed suit when they saw similar advantages for supporting a central bank. The idea was that when the shocks of instability come, the central banks would simply loan what was needed to the FRB participants to keep them solvent (and the game of musical chairs going) until the storm passed. And just where would these new central banks get the money to bail out the FRB banks? Are you ready for this? The central banks were allowed to create the money out of thin air! I can't make this stuff up.

The FRB system's additional interventions supported by the nation-states did nothing to fix the systemic problem of FRB, but it did wonders to increase the profits and power of the global financial system. In fact, the FRB system, which began as a profitable fraud supported by European monarchs, ended in the twentieth century as an absolute power over the global money supply. All of this, including the central bank intervention, occurred in America in the twentieth century. To understand how, we must quickly review the chronological highlights of this momentous time period, a period that birthed the Financial Matrix:

1. America was one of the last holdouts resisting the European FRB cartel, but in 1913, it completely surrendered. This was accomplished through three huge moves all in the same year. With the passage of legislation for the Federal Reserve central bank, the Income Tax amendment, and the democratic election of senators, the United States transformed from an *Empire of Freedom* into an *Empire of Finance*.

2. In 1914, World War I began, and it greatly indebted the nation-states to the banking cartel; with the exception of America (which was a late entrant into the war), the combatants on both sides eliminated the gold standard to inflate the money supply without limits to fund the most expensive war in recorded history.

3. World War I was a victory for democracies over monarchies as the Russian czar, German kaiser, Austrio-Hungarian king, and Ottoman sultan were each replaced with more democratic structures, relying not on the personal finances of the monarch, but on the public finances funded by the FRB cartel.

4. After the war, the over expansion of the money supply predictably led to the greatest boom/bust cycle to that time, known as the Great Depression. In late 1929, the FRB system's artificial expansion

of the money supply systematically collapsed. By 1933, 11,000 of the nation's 25,000 banks had failed, wiping out over $140 billion from customers who had entrusted their life savings to these fraudulent institutions.[2]

5. The FRB cartel profited immensely during the booms and increased power immensely during the bust. For instance, during the Great Depression, President Franklin Delano Roosevelt (FDR) took the American dollar off the gold standard nationally, allowing the FRB cartel to further inflate the American dollar.

6. The American people lost confidence in the free market, unaware that the true cause for the instability was inherent within the FRB system. In consequence, the American people surrendered freedoms and the free market, and FDR's New Deal policies centralized society and government on a scale previously unimaginable.

7. World War II centralized and indebted nations even further. At the close of the war, the Bretton Woods agreement mandated that the American dollar backed by gold would be the reserve currency for each nation's central bank in a worldwide FRB banking cartel.

8. In 1971, President Richard Nixon announced the American dollar would no longer be convertible to gold internationally, birthing the Financial Matrix with absolute power over the money supply of the world, no longer backed by gold, but only by political power. The Financial Matrix, in other

words, has an unlimited power to create unlimited
amounts of money at any time.[3]

The Financial Matrix's absolute power over the world's
money supply resulted from the progressive increase in the
financial system's power with each economic emergency. The
1913 creation of the Federal Reserve did many things, but one
thing it certainly did not do was end the boom/bust cycle instability of the money supply. In fact, the massive inflation of the
money supply during World War I and postwar 1920s America
led directly to the massive deflation of the money supply during
the Great Depression.

The fundamental mistake the financial elites made here, in
systems theory, is called *shifting the burden,* where interventions
address symptoms instead of the actual underlying problem.
It's like trying to save a dying tree by trimming leaves instead
of addressing what's happening with its roots. World-renowned
Massachusetts Institute of Technology (MIT) systems scientist
Peter Senge cited alcoholism as an example of shifting the burden, wherein a person drinks to manage deep-seated emotional
issues, but the alcohol only shifts the burden by temporarily allowing the drunk to forget their troubles (at least until morning).

Perhaps the alcohol masks the pain temporarily, but the
underlying problem remains unaddressed. This is the case no
matter how much alcohol is consumed, and the shifting of the
burden culminates in the person now having two issues: the
still-unaddressed emotional pain and a new problem of alcohol
addiction. Likewise, FRB debt-money is the underlying fundamental problem in the world economy, and regardless of how
many interventions the financial elites dream up, the underlying
problem of the gap between total money supply available and
total debts owed remains unaddressed. Therefore, not only are

the central banks wholly incapable of preventing the boom/ bust cycle, they are actually amplifiers of it.[4]

As a result, the central banks' shifting the burden intervention merely allowed the FRB system to inflate further before deflating, causing even bigger boom/bust cycles to occur. The partnership between banks, which greatly increased profits, and governments, which greatly increased power, was paid for by the people's production. This did not escape the notice of the Nobel Prize–winning economist F. A. Hayek, who near the end of his life observed: "The history of government managed money has, except for a few short happy periods, been one of incessant fraud and deception."[5]

This *incessant fraud and deception* led to this: the central banks pyramiding their created money on top of the banking system's fractional reserves, causing the money supply to multiply many times over. Naturally, this intervention failed because it did not address the underlying issue: the instability caused by the gap between the total debt-money supply and total debts. After all, the ability to create more debt-money not only does nothing to close the gap between total debts and the total money supply, but actually increases the gap! In other words, central banks, at best, only delay the inevitable collapse of the boom/bust cycle and, at worst, increase the scope and severity of the crash.

Under the gold standard, the central banks were allowed to fractionally reserve on top of the limited supply of gold. In other words, the central banks turned the gold into ten times as many banknotes, and then the FRB system ten times increased the banknotes. Somehow, the financial elites convinced themselves that the central banks would stabilize a game of musical chairs by increasing the game's size by one hundred times over. The thought apparently was that if a game involving ten chairs and twenty participants was unstable, then using one thousand chairs and two thousand participants would be much better. This is ludicrous logically because the proposed solution does not address the underlying systemic imbalance. And no matter how many times the central banks kick the proverbial can down the road, it's only a matter of time before that can will detonate and blow up the world economy.

Gold Standard Money Pyramid

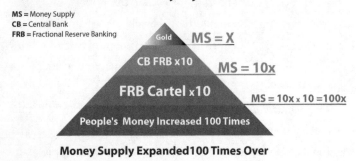

MS = Money Supply
CB = Central Bank
FRB = Fractional Reserve Banking

Gold $MS = X$

CB FRB x10 $MS = 10x$

FRB Cartel x10 $MS = 10x \times 10 = 100x$

People's Money Increased 100 Times

Money Supply Expanded 100 Times Over

This is the situation plaguing society today. Predictably, the boom/bust cycles resulting from this debt-money game are growing in size and severity. This is because with every new financial crisis, the central banks must intervene in increasingly radical ways in order to keep the charade of stability going. Remember, to function properly, the free market requires a stable money supply. Instead, the FRB system and its central bank accomplices create the exact opposite: something resembling an out-of-control Slinky.

Unfortunately, the American political leaders lacked the systems acumen to realize the FRB banking cartel was the root cause of the post–World War I inflationary boom cycle, followed by the corresponding deflation during the Great Depression bust cycle. Thus, instead of eliminating the root cause, the FRB-centralized cartel banking fraud, Roosevelt, and his advisers blamed the monetary failure on the free market system. Thus, they shifted the burden even more, rewarding the financial system by delegating even more power to them, despite them being the root cause of the problem in the first place. In other words, despite the FRB system behaving exactly as systems theory predicted, with the inflation of the money supply followed by a corresponding deflation (as the graphic below clearly displays), FDR gave the FRB cartel even more power by eliminating the gold standard within the American economy during the Great Depression.

Money Supply During The Great Depression Era

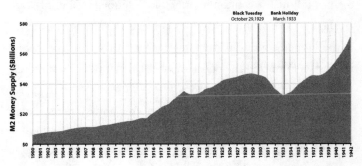

The Great Depression resulted when the money supply deflated after it was artificially inflated by the Federal Reserve and FRB system. It was an economic catastrophe of immense proportions. After all, not only did the banks fraudulently profit during the boom, but the tragic consequences of the bust were passed off mainly to the American people:

From 1929–1933, production at the nation's factories, mines, and utilities fell by more than half. People's real (adjusted for inflation/deflation) disposable incomes dropped 28%. Stock prices collapsed to one-tenth of their pre-crash height. The number of unemployed Americans rose from 1.6 million in 1929 to

12.8 million in 1933. At the height of the Depression, one of every four workers was out of a job.[6]

The American economy was brought to its knees by the FRB system during the Great Depression, and those who caused it (the nation-states and FRB system) were not only not reprimanded, but rewarded. After all, the FRB system was no longer restrained by the gold standard and could now inflate the money supply within the American economy even further to increase its profits and power. Unfortunately, FDR and the New Dealers did not follow the economic principle described by author Henry Hazlitt: "The art of economics consists in looking not merely at the immediate but at the longer effects of any act or policy; it consists in tracing the consequences of that policy not merely for one group but for all groups."[7]

America violated numerous economic and systems theory principles during the Great Depression, and the world economy is still living with the disastrous consequences of the wayward policies. The economic catastrophe, however, led to an even greater ideological one when the ruling elites convinced the people that the free market caused the Great Depression, deflecting blame from the real culprit, the inherent instability of the FRB system.

The Great Depression devastated America because along with the lost jobs was the lost faith in the free market system (to be discussed further in an upcoming chapter). The demoralized people, in effect, demanded that the fox guard the henhouse, surrendering their God-given liberty and property to governmental and financial control, somehow expecting the same people who caused the problem by defrauding the people's money to now fix it by allowing them further power to defraud.

Another factor fueling the growth of the financial system's absolute power over money was the two world wars. Author Randolph Bourne once wrote, "War is the health of the State,"[8] emphasizing that the State grows more in power and resources during warfare than at any other time. After all, the people are whipped into a frenzy in unity against a common enemy and asked to sacrifice for the good of the nation, while the State increases taxes and borrowing to fund the war. The State centralizes the economy as the people willingly surrender their spiritual, political, and economic freedoms in an all-out effort to achieve one thing—namely, victory over the enemy. Throughout history, tyrants have used national emergencies (like the Great Depression and wars) to gain power at the expense of the people's freedoms. People will surrender freedoms when security is endangered, and nothing endangers security as much as war. Moreover, unlimited war requires access to unlimited funding, and in the twentieth century, this money was conveniently provided by the national central banks directing the FRB system. The world wars, in other words, were the key aspect in the Financial Matrix achieving absolute power.

An additional factor in the birth of the Financial Matrix was the effective end of monarchy rule in the West at the close of World War I. The monarchs began as the senior partners in the FRB system fraud, so powerful, in fact, that when debts became excessive to the FRB system, they simply refused to pay. Social justice reformer Shridath Ramphal noted:

> Medieval historians have told the story of the failure of European monarchs to honour debts to Italian banks; Edward III of England was notorious. French kings from the sixteenth to the nineteenth century defaulted with some frequency, every thirty years on average.

Certainly, over the last 500 years there have been regular periods of default.[9]

The senior partners (monarchs) in the FRB fraud, in short, had the unseemly habit of defaulting on their debts, bankrupting some of the banking houses along the way. As a result, from the Renaissance onward, the junior partners (the FRB system) in the fraud sought methods to protect themselves from monarchical whims. And with the advent of modern democracies, the FRB system's method of protection was revealed. After all, the president/prime minister position was only temporarily rented, and not a lifetime position like the monarchy, meaning they were less concerned about running up debts since they would not be responsible to pay them. Moreover, the end of monarchies benefited the banking system, for loans were now owed by the public nations and not private monarchs. Thus, unlike a monarch who had borrowed the money personally, the elected officials borrowed the money publicly; even when they left office, the loans were still the responsibility of the nation. As a result, after World War I, when most nations replaced monarchies with elected and appointed officials, the banking system moved from junior partners in the FRB fraud obedient to kings and queens to senior partners in the FRB fraud directing the finances of obedient nation-states.

Finally, after World War II, the Bretton Woods agreement centralized the world money supply with the American dollar now being the reserve currency for the central banks. Instead of storing gold and practicing fractional reserve banking on top of it, each national central bank stored American dollars created by the American central bank and then FRB pyramided its currency on top of it. In other words, only the American dollar was pegged to the gold supply, and all other national currencies were pegged to the dollar. The central bank's FRB system, despite having completely failed to stabilize the money supply, a failure which led directly to the Great Depression, was after World War II rewarded with complete control over the world's money supply.

Altogether, twentieth-century monetary history is a series of three failures: the FRB system itself, the further central bank intervention, and finally, the total elimination of the gold standard. With each failure, instead of eliminating the underlying FRB systemic issue, the financial elites plowed ahead with further interventions. Strikingly, the third and final intervention was more radical than anything previously imagined. It was as if our binge drinker had switched to consuming pure alcohol. In this case, the figurative straight alcohol meant the complete and worldwide elimination of the gold standard (the connection between money supply in circulation and gold held in reserve). Even though gold's connection with money is nearly as old as recorded history and was the last tether to fiscal sanity, it was completely discarded in 1971. Central banks originally created money with fractional gold reserves to backstop the FRB system, ensuring that money was at least somewhat limited by the physical gold supply. However, as the global FRB system continued to falter, gold, the last vestige of rationality and the final limitation on the financial system's absolute power, was terminated. From now on, the American dollar became a total fiat (by government mandate) money. Interestingly, it was done by the US president who famously stated, "I am not a crook."

Camp David Retreat: The End of the World Gold Standard

In 1971, President Richard Nixon was stuck, and America was on the verge of bankruptcy. Under duress, Nixon summoned a Camp David weekend retreat to discuss with his financial advisers the emergency and potential options to address it. The fateful decision from this weekend transformed the world's money system and birthed the global Financial Matrix.

Although one of the world's two superpowers, America was unable to pay for its expanding welfare and warfare commitments. The Land of Liberty was caught between the financial *rock and a hard place* – the lust for unlimited power constrained by the limited money supply. On one hand (the *rock*), if America continued to expand the money supply through dollar inflation, foreign nations would redeem these inflated dollars for gold, exposing America's bankruptcy by depleting its gold supply. This would embarrass America internationally and is the reason Nixon called the emergency financial summit. On the other hand (the *hard place*), if America didn't expand the money supply through dollar inflation, it could not move forward financially because without free money creation, taxes would instead be needed to pay for everything, and the people would never freely agree to the massive increase that would be required. Nixon and his cronies were in a financial pinch, the same pinch all of us experience when we realize our parents were right that money doesn't grow on trees. This realization led us to budget, prioritize, and carefully allocate our limited funds in a responsible manner. Ideally, governments must balance budgets and manage their funds responsibly just like the rest of us. They can do this by either cutting expenses or raising taxes. But Nixon refused to do either. The president and his Camp David advisers evidently reasoned that the most powerful nation in the world should not be limited in its power by a limited money supply.

The American government during the Great Depression had already eliminated gold convertibility rights (the ability to redeem paper dollars for their equivalent in gold) for US citizens. This gave the American government and Big Bank cartel the right to rob from US citizens, but Nixon's gang was contemplating canceling gold convertibility rights for foreign nations, providing the Financial Matrix the right to rob the citizens of the world. Unbelievably, the American government wanted to borrow money so badly that it allowed the Federal Reserve to inflate the American dollar without any limitations from the gold reserves. This meant the world's money supply could be inflated without limit, since the American dollar is used as the reserve currency for every central bank in the world. The central banks, in other words, could now pyramid their nation's money on top of an American dollar without any physical limits. This did more than just disconnect money from gold; it also disconnected money from economic reality. Money would no longer be a limited quantity regulated by the amount of gold on hand; instead, it would now be an unlimited quantity regulated only by the whims of the Federal Reserve. On August 15, 1971, Nixon announced that, in fact, the American dollar would now grow on trees, becoming forevermore a completely fiat money (money backed, not by precious metals as before, but now by government legal tender laws mandating its use), without gold convertibility rights. The Camp David alchemists rubbed Aladdin's lamp, directed the Federal Reserve genie to produce unlimited dollars for America's federal government on demand, and banished budgeting forever.

America ignored economic law and initiated the age of money tied to nothing for the global economy. The graphic below displays just how quickly the money supply exploded after 1971, when the financial elites were given the power to create an unlimited amount of fiat dollars. Economist Ludwig von Mises warned, "Just as the sound money policy of gold standard advocates went hand in hand with liberalism, free trade, capitalism and peace, so is inflationism part and parcel of imperialism, militarism, protectionism, statism and socialism."[10]

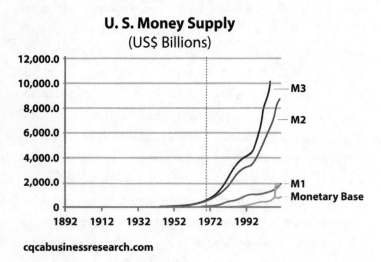

U. S. Money Supply
(US$ Billions)

cqcabusinessresearch.com

However, scarcity is a truth that cannot be rescinded by any earthly power just because it says so. After all, there are no free lunches, only the unjust power to force others to pay for them. Sure, the big banks have received trillions in newly created Federal Reserve dollars for funding the out-of-control American State, but the trillions of new dollars created by the FRB system are what created the debt deluge discussed in Chapter 1. The Financial Matrix creates money out of thin air and then loans it to society (the people, businesses, and governments of the world), who now must work (expend human energy) to pay back the principal and interest. In other words, the banks create something out of nothing, they loan the nothing to societies wanting something, and the people must then earn something to pay back the nothing. In consequence, the big banks became wealthy beyond their wildest imaginings, the federal governments became powerful beyond their wildest dreams, but the world became indebted beyond its worst nightmares. The Camp David cabal birthed something new, something global, and something sinister.

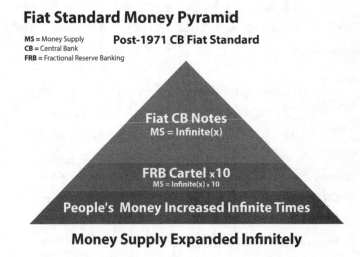

Fiat Standard Money Pyramid

MS = Money Supply
CB = Central Bank
FRB = Fractional Reserve Banking

Post-1971 CB Fiat Standard

Fiat CB Notes
MS = Infinite(x)

FRB Cartel x10
MS = Infinite(x) x 10

People's Money Increased Infinite Times

Money Supply Expanded Infinitely

Without the gold standard, the Money Pyramid is unlimited because it is built on a fiat standard. Of course, the Financial Matrix fiat system will collapse as all other fiat-money experiments have, but since the American dollar is now the fiat monetary base for the world's money supply, the collapse will be global in scale. However, its eventual collapse will provide an opportunity to free all nations from the oppressive fiat-standard Financial Matrix financial system. After all, the collapse of tyranny is an opportunity for liberty and justice, as economist Ludwig von Mises explained:

The collapse of an inflation policy carried to its extreme—as in the United States in 1781 and in France in 1796— does not destroy the monetary system, but only the credit money or fiat money of the State that has overestimated the effectiveness of its own policy. The collapse emancipates commerce from etatism (Statism) and establishes metallic money again.[11]

The 2008 financial crisis, according to the Financial Crisis Inquiry Commission, nearly collapsed the world economy. They explained:

> For example, as of 2007, the five major investment banks—Bear Stearns, Goldman Sachs, Lehman Brothers, Merrill Lynch, and Morgan Stanley—were operating with extraordinarily thin capital. By one measure, their leverage ratios were as high as 40 to 1, meaning for every $40 in assets, there was only $1 in capital to cover losses. Less than a 3% drop in asset values could wipe out a firm. To make matters worse, much of their borrowing was short-term, in the overnight market—meaning the borrowing had to be renewed each and every day. . . . And the leverage was often hidden—in derivatives positions, in off-balance-sheet entities, and through "window dressing" of financial reports available to the investing public.[12]

Twelve short years later, the 2020 monetary collapse was even greater, and this is before the COVID-19 quarantine costs are added in. Perhaps the growth in the Federal Reserve's total assets is the best indicator of the FRB system's complete monetary failure. In an effort to prop up the insolvent banks during the bust cycle, the Federal Reserve must buy the high-priced inflated assets (called *toxic assets*) to provide liquidity (money injections) to protect the banks. Further, it buys these practically worthless assets to clear them from the bank's books, allowing the banks to reset themselves without having to declare bankruptcy like the people do who defaulted on the properties. In other words, the people go bankrupt during the bust cycle, but the central banks ensure the FRB system, the source of the boom/bust cycle, remains unscathed. Of course, none of these central bank shenanigans can protect the systematically insolvent FRB system; instead, they can only delay the bust cycle by continuing the boom (injecting further money into the FRB system), increasing the size of the final bust cycle when it finally rebalances the hopelessly imbalanced system.

Twentieth-century monetary history confirms the importance of thinking systematically because the theory has predicted the actual outcomes with impressive predictability. After all, the Federal Reserve went from around $100 billion in total assets for the first fifty-eight years of its existence (when the gold standard held it in check) to over $1 trillion in the next thirty-seven years (until the 2008 financial crisis), and then to over $6 trillion in the next twelve years, and they are estimated to surpass $9 trillion before the 2020 banking collapse is rehabilitated. The Federal Reserve is the wealthiest entity in the world, the heart of the Financial Matrix, and owns all of these assets with money created out of thin air. There is no greater absolute power imaginable, and yet it is still unable to stabilize the unstablizable FRB system.

Balance Sheet of the Federal Reserve:
Total Assets (1914 – 4/13/2020)

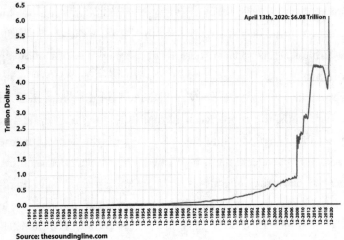

Source: thesoundingline.com

The 2020 COVID-19 quarantine, in other words, misdirected the people's attention away from yet another complete collapse of the FRB system while compounding the world's long-term financial pain. Interestingly, the COVID-19 crisis, although greatly damaging the long-term economic prospects for the people and governments, actually benefited the banking system. After all, the government flowed trillions of dollars into their coffers; the federally enhanced unemployment benefits (an extra $600 per week) and mortgage forbearance plans ensured the FRB system didn't completely collapse. Without these measures, according to the chief economist for Moody's Analytics, Mark Zandi, an estimated 30% of American home loans would have defaulted (about 15 million households), which would have completely collapsed the highly leveraged FRB system. This explains why the financial elites keep publicly proclaiming how strong the banking system is, as former Federal Reserve Chair Janet Yellen did in April 2020 on CNBC: "We have a strong, well capitalized banking system." [13] Despite these soothing words, and others from Federal Reserve Chair Jerome Powell and US Treasury Secretary Steven Mnuchin, to name a few, the fractional reserve banks are systemically sick. In 2020, Wall Street veteran Pam Martens observed:

> . . . the public is increasingly getting curious as to why the New York Fed has had to pump a cumulative $9 trillion in cash to these Wall Street banks, since September 17 of last year, if they are so well capitalized. Can big banks actually be well capitalized and have no liquid money to make loans—the key function of a bank? As we have regularly noted, the Fed's trillions of dollars in cash infusions to the banks began months before there was any coronavirus COVID-19 outbreak anywhere in the world.[14]

Hegel spoke an unfortunate truth when he noted, "We learn from history that we do not learn from history."[15] Throughout the history of debt-money interventions in the free market economy, the absolute power displayed by the Financial Matrix, though increasingly radical at each step, did nothing to teach the financial elites of the danger of their scheme. In fact, as the following bar chart reveals, the gap between total debts and total money supply is expanding annually, and although the day of reckoning can be delayed with further debt, it will not be denied. And when the gap between total debts and the total money supply becomes unpayable, the entire debt structure will implode in a flurry of defaults. Ultimately, the Financial Matrix is a snake that swallows its own tail. As Longfellow once wrote, "Whom the gods would destroy, they first make go mad."

In 1971, the American dollar went from pegged to gold with all other currencies pegged to it to a mere fiat dollar with the ability to create trillions with a snap of a finger, as Federal Reserve Chair Jerome Powell admitted:

> We print it digitally. So as a central bank, we have the ability to create money digitally. And we do that by buying Treasury Bills or bonds or other government guaranteed securities. And that actually increases the money supply. We also print actual currency and we distribute that through the Federal Reserve banks.[16]

The money supply has exploded since 1971 (as the bar chart shows), but the total debts, predictably, have grown even faster. The Financial Matrix is a legal counterfeiter, even though anyone else attempting to do the same thing would be criminally prosecuted. And, as the bar chart conveys, the underlying FRB system is still not resolved; in fact, it's exponentially worse, despite giving absolute power to the Financial Matrix.

Monetary Regimes & Price Inflation
(Price Deflation Was Common Before the Fed Was Established)

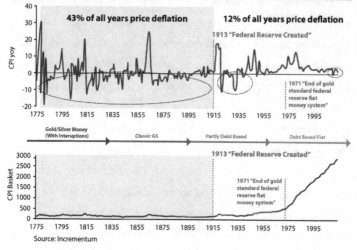

Source: Incrementum

The effects of inflation are revealed in the Consumer Price Index (CPI), which is a weighted average of prices of a basket of consumer goods and services, items like transportation, food, and medical care. The CPI is a tool to track periods of inflation and deflation. As the CPI increases, the people's wealth decreases due to inflation. The preceding CPI chart visually displays the growth in worldwide inflation. Before the Federal Reserve, each expansion of the money supply (inflation) was quickly followed by a contraction (deflation) to rebalance it to its original levels. This ensured the prices paid by consumers, although fluctuating slightly during inflation/deflation cycles, remained fairly consistent from 1775 to 1913. However, with the creation of the Federal Reserve in 1913, inflation began to greatly outrun deflation, and after 1971 (with the elimination of the gold standard), deflation has been practically nonexistent. The end result is the

FRB system now profits during inflation, but is protected by the central banks printing more money to protect against deflation. This saddles consumers with consistently higher prices while it secures consistently higher profits for the Financial Matrix. The CPI data confirms this as it doubled shortly after the introduction of the Federal Reserve and then doubled again after the United States was nationally taken off the gold standard during the 1930s. Since 1971, however, the CPI index has been a runaway freight train with the removal of the gold standard internationally. The middle class has been utterly annihilated. The final shifting the burden, the termination of gold redemption to foreign nations, exploded the CPI for the people and the absolute power of the Financial Matrix. It's doubtful Lord Acton had the Financial Matrix in mind when he warned, "Absolute power corrupts absolutely." [17] Nevertheless, even the absolute power of money creation given to the Federal Reserve cannot stop the ever-widening cyclical swings caused by the unaddressed underlying FRB systemic instability. In 1990, MIT Senior Lecturer Peter Senge explained how developing world governments shift the burden financially, and that explanation is an exact description of Federal Reserve actions in 2020:

> A Third World nation, unable to face difficult choices in limiting government expenditures in line with its tax revenues, finds itself generating deficits that are financed through printing money and inflation. Over time, inflation becomes a way of life, more and more government assistance is needed, and chronic deficits become accepted as inevitable. [18]

Thirty years ago, what was considered immoral behavior of small-country tyrants has now become the accepted worldwide central bank policy. Be that as it may, it's important not to throw out the baby with the bathwater. After all, banking is a vital aspect of the free market system under liberty and justice for all. The key is to ensure the banks play by the same rules that all other businesses are supposed to play by. For instance, bankers are matchmakers that connect entities who have money to those who need money. In a free market, banking produces a return on investment (ROI) by paying depositors interest for surrendering a portion of their deposits for a period of time. This money is then loaned to other customers who pay a higher rate of interest. If the bank pays 3% interest to depositors but earns 9% interest from borrowers, then the bank's gross ROI is 300%—not a bad ROI before expenses for a business. The FRB system, however, according to the US Department of Commerce, revealed in 2008 that the American banking system paid depositors $178.6 billion in total interest while earning a whopping $3.29 trillion on total loans. This is a preposterous 1,842% ROI, which means the FRB system had gross returns over eighteen times greater than the money invested! Monopoly profits are always exorbitant, but when the Financial Matrix makes trillions from billions, every other monopoly is left in the dust. Even after accounting for other bank expenses, an 1,842% ROI is why the banking system pays the highest executive bonuses and owns the biggest and best buildings in town.

President Nixon gave the Financial Matrix control of the world's money supply through the privately owned Federal Reserve, which is neither federal nor has any reserves, and it's been all downhill for liberty and justice ever since. In 2020, the Financial Matrix's power is so absolute that the Federal Reserve created over $4 trillion in a matter of months to protect the FRB system, while the world's wealthiest person in 2020, Jeff Bezos, is *only* worth around $200 billion after a lifetime of entrepreneurship. There is no entity as powerful as the Federal Reserve, and it is merely one of the central bank cogs in the Financial Matrix wheel. Whereas it took the IRS, and its nearly 75,000 agents, countless man hours to collect around $2 trillion in 2019, Jerome Powell created more money than that several times over in mere nanoseconds. Before the Camp David disaster, the financial powers enjoyed immense power, but according to internationally renowned historian and Washington, DC, insider Carroll Quigley:

> The powers of financial capitalism had another far-reaching aim, nothing less than to create a world system of financial control in private hands able to dominate the political system of each country and the economy of the world as a whole. This system was to be controlled in a feudalist fashion by the central banks of the world acting in concert.[19]

After Camp David, in other words, the Financial Matrix achieved its goal of running the global economy, with the people of the world becoming debt serfs to the feudalist financial lords. The Financial Matrix has achieved absolute power over the fiat money supply, a form of fool's gold forced on society by the nation-state's power. And he who controls the fool's gold, controls the fools.

Every lie we tell incurs a debt to the truth. Sooner or later that debt is paid.

—Valery Legasov in *Chernobyl* documentary

CHAPTER 4

Money, Media, Management, and Monopolies

Social order can only be achieved in one of two basic ways: the first being the Golden Rule, "Do unto others as you would have them do unto you," which contains the underlying principles of a just society; or the second being the Power Rule, "Do unto others what you have the power to do," which contains the underlying principles of an unjust society, one in which the powerful are able to plunder others without suffering adverse consequences for doing so. With these two poles of human society in view, we can cut through the otherwise complicated and distracting myriad theories on government, economics, and social order, and realize that society is ultimately based on Golden Rule production or Power Rule plunder. Economist Frédéric Bastiat broke down how production and plunder play out within society:

> This question of legal plunder must be settled once and for all, and there are only three ways to settle it:
>
> 1. The few plunder the many.
> 2. Everybody plunders everybody.
> 3. Nobody plunders anybody.[1]

The first option is an injustice where the elites plunder the masses, the second option is a lawless anarchy where everyone is potentially plundered, and the third option is liberty and justice for all. The dismal record of civilizations that built on the first two of Bastiat's plunder choices (option one chosen by ancient Egypt and the late Roman Empire or option two, civil war anarchy of the ancient Greeks and Renaissance Italy city-states) predictably led to oppression, injustice, and their eventual collapse. The third choice, however, despite being extremely rare, and normally not enduring for more than a generation or two, produced societies in which people could rise on merits and not titles, classes, or creeds. In fact, everywhere we see justice and liberty uplifted and plunder punished by law, society has flourished in creativity, production, and wealth.

Historically, anytime and anywhere absolute power has been achieved it behaves like a giant star with a magnetic field capable of centralizing every other societal function within its orbit. And like a star's magnetic field, absolute power in human action cannot be turned off once turned on. All inferior powers quickly align with the absolute power to secure perks and positions inside the ruling clique, whereas those who resist suffer excommunication. This hierarchy of subordinate allies, consisting of retainers, bureaucrats, and intellectuals, serves the absolute power to enjoy subordinated power and perks. In the Politics of Obedience, Étienne de La Boétie describes how it only takes five or six committed retainers to subject an entire country to an absolute dictator's bureaucracy:

> These six manage their chief so successfully that he comes to be held accountable not only for his own misdeeds but even for theirs. The six have six hundred who profit under them, and with the six hundred they

do what they have accomplished with their tyrant. The six hundred maintain under them six thousand, whom they promote in rank, upon whom they confer the government of provinces or the direction of finances . . . [2]

This is why absolute power always grows because everywhere it turns, it finds lackeys who are, according to La Boétie,

. . . wooing and begging his favor, and doing much more than he tells them to do. Such men must not only obey orders; they must anticipate his wishes; to satisfy him they must foresee his desires; they must wear themselves out, torment themselves, kill themselves with work in his interest, and accept his pleasure as their own, neglecting their preference for his, distorting their character and corrupting their nature; they must pay heed to his words, to his intonation, to his gestures, and to his glance. Let them have no eye, nor foot, nor hand that is not alert to respond to his wishes or to seek out his thoughts.[2]

Once absolute power is unleashed upon such a civilization, like a supernova star it brings everything into its orbit, burning brightly temporarily, but in the end, collapsing upon its own weight. Every supernova, despite how brightly it shines, burns out in the end. Why does absolute power always end badly? For one thing, it behaves like an addictive drug that destroys the character and even the sanity of those who wield it. For another, since the human heart has both good and evil susceptibilities, absolute power cannot be entrusted to anyone, regardless of how noble the people or entity thinks they are, because it will reveal the evil within. Aleksandr Solzhenitsyn summarized the challenge: "If only there were evil people somewhere insidiously committing evil deeds, and it were necessary only to separate them from the rest of us and destroy them. But the line dividing good and evil cuts through the heart of every human being."[3] This is why absolute power destroys justice and liberty, because when any human institution achieves unlimited power, it's only a matter of time before evil tempts the all-powerful to plunder people because they can do so without painful consequences. Frédéric Bastiat described the phenomenon:

> Man can live and satisfy his wants only by ceaseless labor; by the ceaseless application of his faculties to natural resources. This process is the origin of property. But it is also true that a man may live and satisfy his wants by seizing and consuming the products of the labor of others. This process is the origin of plunder. Now since man is naturally inclined to avoid pain—and since labor is pain in itself—it follows that men will resort to plunder whenever plunder is easier than work. History shows this quite clearly. And under these conditions, neither religion nor morality can stop it. When, then, does plunder stop? It stops when it becomes more painful and more dangerous than labor. It is evident, then, that the proper purpose of law is to use the power of its collective force to stop this fatal tendency to plunder instead of to work. All the measures of the law should protect property and punish plunder. But, generally, the law is made by one man or one class of men. And since law cannot operate without the sanction and support of a dominating force, this force must be entrusted to those who make the laws. This fact, combined with the

fatal tendency that exists in the heart of man to satisfy his wants with the least possible effort, explains the almost universal perversion of the law. Thus it is easy to understand how law, instead of checking injustice, becomes the invincible weapon of injustice. It is easy to understand why the law is used by the legislator to destroy in varying degrees among the rest of the people, their personal independence by slavery, their liberty by oppression, and their property by plunder. This is done for the benefit of the person who makes the law, and in proportion to the power that he holds.[1]

Bastiat wrote these words in 1848, but few since have expressed so poignantly why absolute power is such an anathema to liberty and justice. Bastiat, however, spoke about the absolute power of the state, the monopoly of force within society, but the Financial Matrix is an international absolute money power. And once the international financial elites gained absolute power over the money supply, the complete centralization of formerly free nations and the eventual collapse of Western civilization were the predictable outcomes.

For example, the Financial Matrix was the natural consequence of the 1971 termination of the gold standard, which gave the Federal Reserve–led FRB cartel absolute power over the money supply. Once this was achieved, the subordinate powers quickly fell into its orbit. Like a supernova, the Financial Matrix has drawn every nation-state into its power structure following a pattern that can best be described by the alliteration of Money, Media, Management, and Monopolies. Everywhere absolute power has been achieved historically, we see the same supernova pattern. The centralized mass draws everything into itself until it eventually becomes too large, at which point it explodes into a supernova temporarily before imploding into a blackhole. Similarly, the Financial Matrix supernova exploded in the twentieth century but will implode in the twenty-first. Just as the supernova cannot endure, neither can absolute power in human institutions because it has a highly volatile nature.

Before its ultimate destruction, while it's still burning brightly, absolute power grows into a monopsony: a situation where there is only one buyer who determines the value of everything. Whoever serves the absolute power monopsony advances and whoever doesn't is discarded. Thus, anyone desiring promotion and advancement must do its bidding, falling in line with the ideology of its power orbit. This means that those who participate must surrender ethical principles in order to ride the absolute power's momentum. Those who refuse to surrender their principles are left with only two choices: quietly exit the scene or actively resist. In either scenario, they sacrifice perks to maintain principles, whereas the sellouts sacrifice principles to maintain perks. The fast-trackers drawn into absolute power's orbit must accordingly fall in line with its precepts and begin *singing the company song,* as it were.

While many suggest monolithic conspiracies to account for the global loss of liberty and justice, the truth is probably less astonishing. After all, throughout history absolute power has always led to monopsonies, which naturally draw power seekers, like bugs to light, who seek to sell their services. Those hungry for power and perks quickly ascertain that they must align themselves with the monopsony's ruling ideology and support its objectives in order to advance. The difference between the Financial Matrix and previous absolute powers, however, is the Financial Matrix is the first one that is worldwide in scope. As a worldwide absolute power monopoly/monopsony, the Financial Matrix is drawing power seekers around the globe into its orbit, and they either promote its agenda (the financial plunder of people) or will not advance. Talented people serving the Financial Matrix, even if they know what the Financial Matrix is doing is wrong, must either serve the system or be cast aside. Moreover, as its absolute power draws more areas of society into its orbit, the fast-trackers in every field affected must make a similar choice. The result is an army of faithful lieutenants, in numerous occupations, orbiting around the Financial Matrix's absolute power, willing to professionally advance its monetary worldview to personally advance.

The pull of power and perks is so strong, in fact, that many who previously opposed its enticements eventually succumb to it. For instance, Alan Greenspan was outspoken in his opposition to the fiat money system, proclaiming in a 1966 article: "In the absence of the gold standard, there is no way to protect savings from confiscation through inflation. There is no safe store of value. If there were, the government would have to make its holding illegal, as was done in the case of gold."[4] This is one of the strongest statements against the Financial Matrix's absolute power on record; nonetheless, after he was offered the Chair of the Federal Reserve in the mid-1980s, the former strident critic for the next twenty years became an avid promoter of the worldwide fiat money system.

Media

Once the Financial Matrix achieved absolute power in this way, it followed that the Media elites—the elites directing the public schools, universities, foundations, social media, newspapers, movies, magazines, television, etc.—only promoted members who actively supported the ruling paradigm. What resulted is today's self-reinforcing cycle of powerful figures parroting the agreed-upon doctrines until they are the only publicly acceptable opinions. The Financial Matrix won by gaining the support of the intellectuals, and the intellectuals won by supporting the Financial Matrix. As Austrian economist Joseph Salerno described:

> The ruling class, however, confronts one serious and ongoing problem: how to persuade the productive majority, whose tribute or taxes it consumes, that its laws, regulations, and policies are beneficial; that is, that they coincide with "the public interest" or are designed to promote "the common good" or to optimize "social welfare." Given its minority status, failure to solve this problem exposes the political class to serious consequences.[5]

The Media is relied upon to sell the masses on the benefits of following the current power structure. This means that, of necessity, the Media is not really about sharing total truths and facts, as it masquerades. Instead, to borrow a term from Plato, the Media is tasked with sharing "noble lies" in order to justify the absolute power of the Financial Matrix over the people who do the producing. The Media can raise any issues or cause divisions among the people on any grounds so long as the Financial Matrix's absolute power is itself never scrutinized.

Journalist Ryan Grim, in a 2009 article titled *Priceless: How the Federal Reserve Bought the Economics Profession,* described how the Federal Reserve has essentially bought the collective voice of modern economists since, not surprisingly, the mid-1970s (soon after the Financial Matrix achieved its absolute power over money):

The Federal Reserve, through its extensive network of consultants, visiting scholars, alumni and staff economists, so thoroughly dominates the field of economics that real criticism of the central bank has become a career liability for members of the profession, an investigation by the Huffington Post has found. This dominance helps explain how, even after the Fed failed to foresee the greatest economic collapse since the Great Depression, the central bank has largely escaped criticism from academic economists. . . . One critical way the Fed exerts control on academic economists is through its relationships with the field's gatekeepers. For instance, at the Journal of Monetary Economics, a must-publish venue for rising economists, more than half of the editorial board members are currently on the Fed payroll—and the rest have been in the past. . . .

"For the economics profession that came out of the [second world] war, the Federal Reserve was not a very important place as far as they were concerned, and their views on monetary policy were not framed by a working relationship with the Federal Reserve. So I would date it to maybe the mid-1970s," says University of Texas economics professor—and Fed critic—James Galbraith. . . . The Fed also doles out millions of dollars in contracts to economists for consulting assignments, papers, presentations, workshops, and that plum gig known as a *visiting scholarship*. A Fed spokeswoman says that exact figures for the number of economists contracted with weren't available. But, she says, the Federal Reserve spent $389.2 million in 2008 on "monetary and economic policy," money spent on

analysis, research, data gathering, and studies on market
structure; $433 million is budgeted for 2009.[6]

The top monetary economists naturally gravitate into the
Federal Reserve's orbit to seek advancement. And, as in any
field, those who please management advance, while those who
do not leave. Robert Auerbach, a former investigator with the
US House Committee on Financial Services, published the book
Deception and Abuse at the Fed in 2008.[7] His research discovered
that in 1992, between the American Economic Association
(AEA) and the National Association for Business Economics
(NABE), there were approximately 1,000 to 1,500 monetary
economists working in America, and over 500 of them, at any
one time, were employed by the Federal Reserve. And when
those who previously worked for the Fed are added in, practically every major contributor in the monetary economics field is
orbiting around the Fed. Furthermore, many of the editors of
prominent academic journals are on the Fed's payroll. In fact,
it's common practice for a journal editor to review submissions
dealing with Fed policy while also receiving a salary from the
Fed. In 2008, the Huffington Post discovered that 84 of the top
190 editorial board positions for the top seven journals were
connected to the Federal Reserve in some way. Naturally, because the journals determine which economic ideas are respect-
able and which economists are tenured, few articles critical of
Fed policies are published, and none that would dare question
the Fed's existence.[6]

Again, this is the natural response to absolute power because every other power in society orbits around it, choosing
not to bite the hand that feeds it, but rather contribute to it. We
see the same phenomenon in every field. For instance, the key
medical journals now orbit the pharmaceutical cartel, and the

journals will not bite the hand of Big Pharma. Another example would be the federally funded educational system that uses the judicial system to enforce its uniform worldview upon all public schools, squashing any dissent.

Similar scenarios are playing out in many fields orbiting around the Financial Matrix, where the philosophy for advancement in bureaucracies is one must go along to get along. Ryan Grim described the benefits for being in the Fed's good graces:

> Being on the Fed payroll isn't just about the money, either. A relationship with the Fed carries prestige; invitations to Fed conferences and offers of visiting scholarships with the bank signal a rising star or an economist who has arrived. Affiliations with the Fed have become the oxygen of academic life for monetary economists. "It's very important, if you are tenure track and don't have tenure, to show that you are valued by the Federal Reserve," says Jane D'Arista, a Fed critic and an economist with the Political Economy Research Institute at the University of Massachusetts, Amherst. And while most academic disciplines and top-tier journals are controlled by some defining paradigm, in an academic field like poetry, that situation can do no harm other than to, perhaps, a forest of trees. Economics, unfortunately, collides with reality—as it did with the Fed's incorrect reading of the housing bubble and failure to regulate financial institutions. Neither was a matter of incompetence, but both resulted from the Fed's unchallenged assumptions about the way the market worked.[6]

Salerno, quoted earlier, went on to explain how intellectuals are rewarded for providing ideological support for the ruling paradigm of the Financial Matrix:

> Here is where the intellectuals come in. It is their task to convince the public to actively submit to State rule because it is beneficial to do so, or at least to passively endure the State's depredations because the alternative is anarchy and chaos. In return for fabricating an ideological cover for its exploitation of the masses of subjects or taxpayers, these "court intellectuals" are rewarded with the power, wealth, and prestige of a junior partnership in the ruling elite. Whereas in pre-industrial times these apologists for State rule were associated with the clergy, in modern times—at least since the Progressive Era in the U.S.—they have been drawn increasingly from the academy. Politicians, bureaucrats, and those whom they subsidize and privilege within the economy thus routinely trumpet lofty ideological motives for their actions in order to conceal from the exploited and plundered citizenry their true motive of economic gain.[5]

The *court intellectuals* are free to criticize anything and everything except the rule of the Financial Matrix. Those who go along are rewarded, and those who do not are not. Again, no monolithic conspiracy is needed to make all other power centers obey the absolute power. After all, people like healthy salaries and preferential perks in any field. It follows naturally, then, that top leaders in the financial, corporate, charitable, entertainment, education, and journalism fields would similarly desire to benefit from the Financial Matrix's perks and rewards.

Rob Johnson, a former top economist for the United Nations and US Senate Committee on Banking, Housing, and Urban Affairs, said consulting gigs should not be looked at "like it's a payoff, like money. I think it's more being one of, part of, a club—being respected, invited to the conferences, having a hearing with the chairman, having all the prestige dimensions, as much as a paycheck."[6] The Fed's hiring of so many economists can be looked at from several vantage points, Johnson said. "You can look at it from a telescope, either direction. One, you can say well they're reaching out, they've got a big budget and what they're doing, I'd say, is canvassing as broad a range of talent," he says. "You might call that the 'healthy hypothesis.'"[6] However, the other hypothesis, Johnson noted, "is that they're essentially using taxpayer money to wrap their arms around everybody that's a critic and therefore muffle or silence the debate. And I would say that probably both dimensions are operative, in reality."[6] The real problem, again, is absolute power itself. It has made dissension very difficult because anyone with competing ideas is cast into oblivion. This is why absolute power is so dangerous; it expands indefinitely until the host civilization collapses from the lack of competition and innovation.

In the meantime, while absolute power reigns, the *experts* are rewarded for influencing the people's thoughts and actions. Sometimes this influence takes the form of overt manipulation. Walter Lippmann, two-time Pulitzer Prize–winning journalist, said the masses were a "great beast" and "bewildered herd" who needed direction. He even coined the cynical term "manufacture of consent" to explain how to manipulate public opinion:

> That the manufacture of consent is capable of
> great refinements no one, I think, denies. The process
> by which public opinions arise is certainly no less

intricate than it has appeared in these pages, and the opportunities for manipulation open to anyone who understands the process are plain enough. . . . As a result of psychological research, coupled with the modern means of communication, the practice of democracy has turned a corner. A revolution is taking place, infinitely more significant than any shifting of economic power. . . . Under the impact of propaganda, not necessarily in the sinister meaning of the word alone, the old constants of our thinking have become variables.[8]

The end result, as Media critic Noam Chomsky explained, is the specialized intellectual class stampeding the bewildered herd into supporting policies against the people's liberty and justice:

Now there are two "functions" in a democracy: The specialized class, the responsible men, carry out the executive function, which means they do the thinking and planning and understand the common interests. Then, there is the bewildered herd, and they have a function in democracy too . . . they're allowed to say, "We want you to be our leader" or "We want you to be our leader." That's because it's a democracy and not a totalitarian state. That's called an election. But once they've lent their weight to one or another member of the specialized class they're supposed to sink back and become spectators of action, but not participants in a properly functioning democracy.[9]

People, under the banner of democracy, are allowed to participate in the briefest of activities in society, but only in order to pacify them into thinking they are making an authentic contribution—when actually, they are merely choosing between equally dangerous power-hungry manipulators. These *chosen* manipulators, in obedience to the vortex of absolute power, then propagate policies that plunder the very people who elected them. Again: this whole cycle of self-destruction is supported and encouraged by a rapturous Media.

What's worse, not only does the Media play this part in the great deception, but it has also been whittled down to only a few humongous participants, making it easier than ever for the main message in support of the system of absolute power to ring through consistently. For instance, in 1983 author Ben Bagdikian wrote *The Media Monopoly*, in which he stated, "Fifty corporations dominated almost every mass medium." [10] And as if to drive home his point, every time the book was rereleased, the number of corporations dropped, from twenty-nine firms in 1987, to twenty-three in 1990, to fourteen in 1992, to ten in 1997. In fact, according to PBS, five conglomerates dominated the industry by the year 2000. Mark Crispin Miller, a concerned media critic, wrote: "The implications of these mergers for journalism and the arts are enormous. It seems to me that this is, by definition, an undemocratic development. The media system in a democracy should not be inordinately dominated by a few very powerful interests."[11]

Another avenue for undue influence is in the billion-dollar tax-exempt foundations. For example, René Wormser, the general legal counsel for the Reece Committee, an investigative group created by the Eighty-Third Congress, described how foundations were used for political ends. Not only do wealthy donors save billions in taxes, but the power elites serving on the board use funds to promote socialism and other radical policies. Moreover, the Reece Committee identified several colleges and universities that abandoned their sectarian affiliations and charter clauses relating to religion in order to secure endowments from the Carnegie Corporation. Wormser's research concluded:

> An 'élite' has thus emerged, in control of gigantic financial resources operating outside of our democratic processes, which is willing and able to shape the future of this nation and of mankind in the image of its own value concepts. . . . In my opinion, because of death taxes and other taxes, it seems inevitable that much of the wealth of these families ended up in powerful institutions used for societal change. . . . In fifty or a hundred years, a great part of American industry will be controlled by pension and profit-sharing trusts and foundations and a large part of the balance by insurance companies and labor unions. . . . It may be that we will in this manner reach some form of society similar to socialism.[12]

Absolute Power Orbit

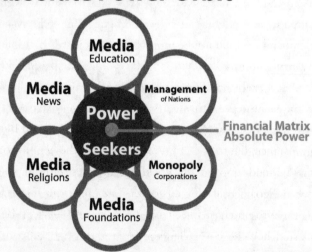

The visual displays how absolute power draws power seekers from every major field into its orbit to centralize the control over society.

One of the essential aspects of this power is its control over media and education. Let's consider exactly why the centralized Media and its blind adherence to the precepts of the absolute power matrix are so dangerous to the people. The Media inundates people with prepackaged views, telling them what to believe, creating preconceived perceptions of reality to manipulate thoughts and actions. The people, like mushrooms, are kept in the dark and periodically fed ongoing loads of manure. No wonder people support so many initiatives contrary to their best interests.

For example, 1913 was a banner year for propaganda as the Federal Reserve Act, the Income Tax amendment, and the democratic election of Senators were all rabidly supported by the people, even though it would be difficult to conceive of three policies more destructive to the people's liberty and justice. Not coincidentally, mainstream media represented each initiative as a plan to soak the rich and protect the little guy—the exact opposite of what resulted.

Such mass manipulation, so successful in the instance of 1913, was not only acceptable in the opinion of people like Lippmann, but absolutely necessary in order to steer the behavior of the unsuspecting masses. Sadly, Lippmann wasn't alone, and there were many others who believed similarly. Edward Bernays, for instance, the father of *public relations* and the nephew of Sigmund Freud, applied his uncle's techniques without apology, with the goal of altering customers' subconscious minds, causing them to purchase his clients' products and services. Bernays boasted how he controlled the masses through subconscious manipulations in his book *Propaganda*:

The conscious and intelligent manipulation of the organized habits and opinions of the masses is an important element in democratic society. Those who manipulate this unseen mechanism of society constitute an invisible government which is the true ruling power of our country. We are governed, our minds are molded, our tastes formed, our ideas suggested, largely by men we have never heard of. This is a logical result of the way in which our democratic society is organized. Vast numbers of human beings must cooperate in this manner if they are to live together as a smoothly functioning society. Our invisible governors are, in many cases, unaware of the identity of their fellow members in the inner cabinet.[13]

Management

Through its monopoly over Money and its orbiting Media, the Financial Matrix essentially influences democratic elections. After all, the two key things political candidates need in a democracy are Money and Media support, which are both orbiting within the Financial Matrix's gravitational field. The competing political parties must have the support of the Financial Matrix or their bid for Management positions will be stillborn. The key in elections is to keep the people evenly divided. The Right historically has supported conservative values and the Warfare State, while the Left has supported liberal values and the Welfare State. The end result is the people stay divided and state power is further enhanced because, regardless of which party wins, the national government has confirmed the public support for its Warfare/Welfare State. Since 1971, interestingly, the parties are coalescing where it is difficult to detect any meaningful

difference in the party lines. After all, the Financial Matrix vets
the candidates from both sides, as author Noam Chomsky described:

> I mean, what's the elections? You know, two guys,
> same background, wealth, political influence, went to
> the same elite university, joined the same secret society
> where you're trained to be a ruler—they both can
> run because they're financed by the same corporate
> institutions.[14]

The Financial Matrix runs the coin flip and allows us to
call heads or tails, but the results are the same; namely, heads,
it wins, and tails, the people lose. In this way, the Management
of governments falls under Financial Matrix influence, as Antony Sutton, a research fellow at Stanford University's prestigious
Hoover Institute, discovered. For five years, 1968 to 1973, Sutton
received the highest commendations on his research on Western
technology and Soviet economic development, revealing how
the West played the key role in the Soviet Union's military and
technological know-how, and had done so from the very beginning. In 1973, he released *National Suicide: Military Aid to the Soviet Union*,[14] a thoroughly researched work with irrefutable proof
that the Cold War conflicts were not fought to restrain communism but were organized to generate multibillion-dollar arma-
ments contracts, after which he was subsequently let go from
the Hoover Institute and his research was defunded. Evidently,
Sutton's conclusions, that the global financial system centered in
the United States loaned billions of dollars to the Soviet Union
and directly or indirectly armed both sides in the Korean and
Vietnam wars, were too much truth to be allowed.

In a 1972 testimony before Subcommittee VII of the Platform Committee of the Republican Party, Sutton summarized his discoveries:

> In a few words: there is no such thing as Soviet technology. Almost all—perhaps 90–95 percent—came directly or indirectly from the United States and its allies. In effect the United States and the NATO countries have built the Soviet Union. Its industrial and its military capabilities. This massive construction job has taken 50 years. Since the Revolution in 1917. It has been carried out through trade and the sale of plants, equipment and technical assistance.[15]

Sutton's research was astonishing enough, but his conclusions are what led to his exit from the ruling intellectuals supporting the Financial Matrix. After all, it made no sense for the United States to be nearly the sole source of funding for the Soviet Union, its alleged archnemesis. Sutton struggled to understand why the American state would allow its military–industrial complex to fund and build the military technologies and weapons used against American soldiers. The paradox was resolved when Sutton realized he had it backward, and the financial system didn't serve the American state, but rather, the American state served the financial system. Sutton, in short, discovered what I have been communicating in this book—namely, the true rulers of the modern world are not the nation-states, but the Financial Matrix. The American and Soviet states borrowed from the same Financial Matrix to purchase weapons from the same military–industrial complex, in a futile effort to defend their nations. As a result, the Soviet Union went bankrupt, and America became indebted as never before, but the Financial Matrix secured untold wealth and power. National governments are now completely beholden to the Financial Matrix.

Monopoly

Finally, once the Financial Matrix controls the Money, Media, and Management of each nation-state, it can leverage this power to build and expand its worldwide Monopolies. The Financial Matrix partners with the ruling elites of each nation to profit off the people's production through joint collaboration to build national and international monopolies and cartels. Debora Mackenzie, in a *New Scientist* article intriguingly titled *Revealed: The Capitalist Network that Runs the World,* shared how in a study of over forty-three thousand transnational corporations (TNCs), a relatively small number of companies, mainly banks, had a "disproportionate power over the global economy." [15] The study was conducted by three systems theorists at the Swiss Federal Institute of Technology in Zurich and claims to be the first to go beyond ideology to specifically verify a network of power. Through a combination of mathematics, modeling, and mountains of corporate data, the network of ownership and control was mapped out. One of the researchers, James Glattfelder, stated, "Reality is so complex, we must move away from dogma, whether it's conspiracy theories or free-market. Our analysis is reality-based." The empirical research supports the supernova absolute power analogy that draws all other powers—in this case, other corporations—into its orbit like planets around the sun. Mackenzie reported:

> From Orbis 2007, a database listing 37 million companies and investors worldwide, they pulled out all 43,060 TNCs and the shared ownerships linking them.

Then they constructed a model of which companies controlled others through shareholding networks, coupled with each company's operating revenues, to map the structure of economic power. The investigation exposed a core of 1318 companies with interlocking ownerships. Each of the 1318 had ties to two or more other companies, and on average they were connected to 20. What's more, although they represented 20 percent of global operating revenues, the 1318 appeared to collectively own through their shares the majority of the world's large blue chip and manufacturing firms— the "real" economy—representing a further 60 percent of global revenues. When the team further untangled the web of ownership, it found much of it tracked back to a "super-entity" of 147 even more tightly knit companies—all of their ownership was held by other members of the super-entity—that controlled 40 percent of the total wealth in the network.[16]

"In effect, less than 1 percent of the companies were able to control 40 percent of the entire network," says Glattfelder. Most were financial institutions. Now the complete picture is coming into view. It started with absolute power over Money, which led to control of the worldwide Media system. This led naturally to control over the Management of the indebted nation-states, which culminated in Financial Matrix–directed Monopolies and cartels. Absolute power always and everywhere leads to central-ized state and economic powers, in this case orbiting around the Financial Matrix. This is the real reason the rich get richer and the middle class is tanking. The pursuit of monopoly is a prof-itable business strategy, as author Federic C. Howe admitted:

These are the rules of big business. They have superseded the teachings of our parents and are reducible to a simple maxim: Get a monopoly; let society work for you; and remember that the best of all business is politics, for a legislative grant, franchise, subsidy or tax exemption is worth more than a Kimberly or Comstock [gold mines] lode, since it does not require any labor, either mental or physical, for its exploitation.[17]

Financial elites may give lip service to free enterprise principles, but those are applied to the people, not themselves and their supporters. Instead, the elites enjoy monopolies and cartels through political cronyism created by the linkages between the Financial Matrix–controlled nation-states and international corporations. The Financial Matrix likes big monopolies with predictable profits and little risk. The reason they loathe true competition is because *disorderly* competition is not predictable. According to economist Joseph Schumpeter, the "gale of creative destruction" was a "process of industrial mutation that continuously revolutionizes the economic structure from within, incessantly destroying the old one, incessantly creating a new one."[18] Similar to how the Wright brothers beat out a military/ university group in becoming the first to powered flight, the bureaucracies struggle to compete against the nimbler competitors constantly threatening to creatively destroy the old methods and replace them with better ones in the free market. As a result, the Financial Matrix cartels believe if you can't beat them, have the state squash them, shamelessly using state power to prohibit new entrepreneurs from *creatively destroying* them. Through the crushing weight of government regulations and barriers to entry, the smaller startup firms collapsed under the added weight, while the larger established firms were dutifully protected from competition.

After all, the free market is a competition among firms to serve customers, similar to the childhood game King of the Hill. Each participant competes by climbing the hill, knocking off the current *king* by serving customers better, and becomes the new king of the hill. However, because the competition is intense and the free market allows anyone with better ideas to compete, it is difficult for anyone to maintain the king position. Not surprisingly, as a result, the Financial Matrix cartels loathe the free market system, seeking instead for state regulatory oversight to rig the game in the cartels' favor. This has led to the Financial Matrix monopolies and cartels having the top spots of nearly every economic hill through regulatory restraining of new competitors. The international corporate conglomerates are like huge 250-pound King of the Hill participants, who combine forces (work together in cartels) to protect the hilltop from smaller competitors while dividing the spoils. They lobby the nation-states' *monopoly of force* to create laws nationally and use military force internationally to secure the "Kingship" of the Hill. After all, while the 100 pounds of state regulatory oversight is a hindrance for the 250-pound giants, it is a crushing weight for newer 50-pound competitors. Historian Gabriel Kolko explained the political cartel cronyism ". . . was based on the functional unity of major political and business leaders. The business and political elites knew each other, went to the same schools, belonged to the same clubs, married into the same families, shared the same values . . ."[19]

The national elites of each country, in other words, orbit around the Financial Matrix to gain corporate positions and perks within the monopoly/cartel system. The elite monopolies increased government regulations, not, as alleged, to protect the people from monopolies, but to protect the monopolies from competition. Kolko, again, delineated the facts from the fiction:

> Ironically, contrary to the consensus of historians, it was not the existence of monopoly that caused the federal government to intervene in the economy, but the lack of it. . . . Despite the large number of mergers, and the growth in the absolute size of many corporations, the dominant tendency in the American economy at the beginning of [the twentieth] century was toward growing competition. Competition was unacceptable . . . it was not the existence of monopoly that caused the federal government to intervene in the economy, but the lack of it.[19]

To summarize, the Financial Matrix proceeded from Money to Media to Management, finally using state power to build a network of Monopolies and cartels. Those in power over the nation-states' monopoly of force have effectively used the law to regulate industries into monopolies and cartels. This has turned the law from an instrument of justice into an instrument of injustice like Frédéric Bastiat warned:

> The law perverted! The law—and, in its wake, all the collective forces of the nation—the law, I say, not only diverted from its proper direction, but made to pursue one entirely contrary! The law becomes the tool of every kind of avarice, instead of being its check! The law is guilty of that very iniquity which it was its mission to punish! [20]

The law became legalized injustice to support the Financial Matrix monopolies. Economist Mark Perry of American Enterprise Institute produced what some have called the "chart of the century" because it reveals just how costly it is to live under the Monopolies and cartels. On one hand, the government-protected cartels provide the so-called non-tradables, not subject to market competition (hospital stays, medical care, and college tuition), which have increased prices two to three times faster than the rate of inflation. On the other hand, the prices of goods subject to competition (toys, televisions, and mobile phones) have decreased over the past two decades. This clearly shows that free markets and actual competition benefit consumers. In other words, the "More Affordable" lines represent free market pricing, while the "More Expensive" lines represent government-supported cartel pricing.

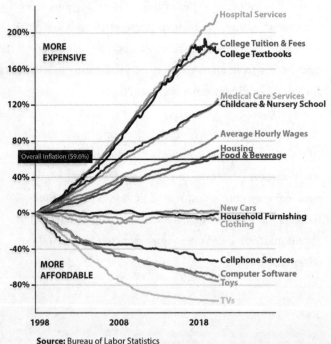

Price Changes (January 1998 to December 2019)
Selected US Consumer Goods & Services, Wages

Source: Bureau of Labor Statistics

As the chart shows, the Financial Matrix has more difficulty internationally where it can't as easily enforce national laws to protect its Monopolies and cartels. Thus, to achieve monopoly-like profits, it must resort to the more ancient and clumsy method of threats and intimidation to plunder the people, backed, if necessary, by military force. Major General Smedley Darlington Butler, one of the most decorated Marines in American history (the only person awarded a Marine Corps Brevet Medal and a Medal of Honor for two separate military actions), was one of the first to express concerns over the military's mafia-like tactics overseas. Butler was an American patriot who served throughout Central America and, at age forty-eight, became one of the Marines' youngest major generals. In a 1933 speech, however, he objected to the misuse of the military: "I wouldn't go to war again as I have done to protect some lousy investment of the bankers. There are only two things we should fight for. One is the defense of our homes and the other is the Bill of Rights. War for any other reason is simply a racket." [21]

After World War I, Butler began questioning US involvement in foreign conflicts because he realized war was less about protecting people and more about protecting profits. Disgusted by the senseless endangerment of military personnel to defend monopoly/cartel profits, he became an unrelenting voice against the business of war:

I spent most of my time being a high class muscleman for Big Business, for Wall Street and for the Bankers. In short, I was a racketeer, a gangster . . . I helped make Mexico and especially Tampico safe for American oil interests in 1914. I helped make Haiti and Cuba a decent place for the National City Bank boys to collect revenues in. I helped in the raping of half a dozen Central American republics for the benefit of Wall Street. I helped purify Nicaragua for the International Banking House of Brown Brothers in 1902–1912. I brought light to the Dominican Republic for the American sugar interests in 1916. I helped make Honduras right for the American fruit companies in 1903. In China in 1927 I helped see to it that Standard Oil went on its way unmolested. Looking back on it, I might have given Al Capone a few hints. The best he could do was to operate his racket in three districts. I operated on three continents.[21]

If anything, the problem is worse today than in Major General Butler's time. For instance, according to CNN, America today has military personnel in 150 countries, indicating the military focus is more offensive than defensive.[22] This is the result of the Financial Matrix capturing the Management of the nation-states' 2 and using the military as its private police force (in this case, paid for by American taxpayers) to protect its international Monopolies and cartels.

Fortunately, there were a few brave spirits who opposed insider groupthink and chose to surrender their positions and perks rather than their principles. Along with Mises, Nock, Bastiat, Sutton, and Butler, who have already been quoted extensively, there were other independent intellectuals like John T. Flynn (who maintained liberty against militarism), Michael Behe (who maintained irreducible complexity against biological naturalism), and Harry Barnes (whose historical revisionism opposed statist propaganda).

These giants advanced quickly in their fields until they became disillusioned by the rank hypocrisy in absolute power promoting consensus over truth. These people, and others like them, were unsung heroes, for they pursued truth for the sake of truth and paid the price. After all, independent thinkers are considered heretics in bureaucratic organizations whose careers must be burned at the stake. The Financial Matrix, like all absolute powers, values obedience over innovation. The last thing it wants is people who dare to think for themselves, which is why anyone who does so is quickly excommunicated.

The Spirit of the Lord is upon me, because he has chosen me to bring good news to the poor. He has sent me to proclaim liberty to the captives and recovery of sight to the blind, to set free the oppressed and announce that the time has come when the Lord will save his people.

—Luke 4:18-19

CHAPTER 5

Force Matrices vs. Free Markets

Now that we have learned these uncomfortable truths about the Financial Matrix's absolute power, we too must choose. For just as the Bible teaches Christians to be wise as serpents but harmless as doves, so must we also be wise to the Financial Matrix's methods and careful not to unwittingly sell out to it. Thankfully, the Financial Matrix money system should collapse in our lifetime, providing a major opportunity to those who desire freedom. Imagine replacing the Financial Matrix with a just money system, one that provides economic, political, and spiritual liberties to all. To achieve this, we must understand the difference between societies built upon Power Rule plunder and those built upon Golden Rule production, while practicing Golden Rule production in our own lives. Nearly every great advance in history has occurred when human beings broke free from the ruling matrices-of-control. In these brief moments, we catch a glimpse of how sweet freedom is when it blossoms into life, liberty, and the security of private property ownership for individuals. It is infinitely valuable, and worthy of our pursuit.

In *The City of God*, the great theologian Augustine said justice is what separates good governments from criminal gangs:

Remove justice, and what are kingdoms but gangs of criminals on a large scale? What are criminal gangs but petty kingdoms? A gang is a group of men under the command of a leader, bound by a compact of association, in which the plunder is divided according to an agreed convention. If this villainy wins so many recruits from the ranks of the demoralized that it acquires territory, establishes a base, captures cities and subdues peoples, it then openly arrogates to itself the title of kingdom, which is conferred on it in the eyes of the world, not by the renouncing of aggression but by the attainment of impunity. For it was a witty and truthful rejoinder which was given by a captured pirate to Alexander the Great. The king asked the fellow, "What is your idea, in infesting the sea?" And the pirate answered, with uninhibited insolence, "The same as yours, in infesting the earth! But because I do it with a tiny craft, I'm called a pirate; because you have a mighty navy, you're called an emperor.[1]

Augustine helps us see that there are two economic paths possible for human civilization, and they are differentiated by ethics. The civilization will either practice: 1) The Power Rule Philosophy (PRP), which is the unethical path (institutionalized injustice) of elite plunder over people whose life, liberty, and property is violated; or 2) The Golden Rule Philosophy (GRP), which is the ethical path (institutionalized justice) of production from people whose life, liberty, and property are protected. Economics, as a result, regardless of the relativistic rhetoric, is anything but morally neutral, for just as a couple can be either pregnant or not pregnant, the people's natural rights are either protected or violated. Neutrality is not an option. As we have seen, the first path, with a few notable exceptions, has been the near-universal economic history of the world, where the powerful use force matrices to plunder the people. The second path, however, has been the dream of the oppressed throughout history, wherein the people's natural rights are protected and production is rewarded within free markets. This dream to live free is encapsulated in the words inscribed on the Statue of Liberty: "Give me your tired, your poor, Your huddled masses yearning to breathe free, The wretched refuse of your teeming shore." Whether a society is just or unjust pivots upon how the government's monopoly of force is applied. As noted previously, the same power used to *organize justice* (the protection of life, liberty, and property) can just as easily, as Augustine stated, be used to "organize injustice" (the taking of life, liberty, and property). Economist Ludwig von Mises used the term "state" to define the governmental power within a specific territory designed to ensure justice: "The state is essentially an apparatus of compulsion and coercion. The characteristic feature of its activities is to compel people through the application or the threat of force to behave otherwise than they would like to behave."[2]

This is the paradox of the state, for any power strong enough to protect rights is also strong enough to violate them. In fact, author Albert Jay Nock distinguished between governments and states, observing that governments were limited powers that protected people's rights, whereas states were unlimited absolute powers that violated them.[3] Following the same distinction, we see the twentieth century in America and Europe as the history of limited-power governments being transformed into absolute-power states. In fact, renowned sociologist Franz Oppenheimer, after more than fifty years of researching nation-states, dismally concluded:

The State . . . is a social institution, forced by a victorious group of men on a defeated group, with the sole purpose of regulating the dominion of the victorious group over the vanquished, and securing itself against revolt from within and attacks from abroad . . . this dominion had no other purpose than the economic exploitation of the vanquished by the victors. No primitive state known to history originated in any other manner.[4]

Throughout history, in other words, the elites have practiced the PRP by capturing the state's absolute power and using it to plunder the people. Nock observed:

In proportion as you give the state power to do things for you, you give it power to do things to you. . . . All the power [the state] has is what society gives it, plus what it confiscates from time to time on one pretext or another; there is no other source from which state power can be drawn.[3]

One of the key aspects to the Power Rule Philosophy is convincing the people that surrendering their freedoms to the state is essential for survival. In reality, however, the surrender of life, liberty, and property is the key to the elite's plunder. The historical dilemma is driven home by French political philosopher Bertrand de Jouvenel, who noted production and plunder were the keys to understanding history:

Whoever does not wish to render history incomprehensible by departmentalizing it—political, economic, social—would perhaps take the view that it is in essence a battle of dominant wills [aristocratic elites], fighting in every way they can for the material which is common to everything they construct: the human labor force [people's production].[5]

After a lifetime of studying power, de Jouvenel concluded that the elites in every generation have sought to control the people's production in order to plunder it. And any time people are economically coerced into doing something against their wills, we are no longer discussing freedom, but rather force.

To profit from their power, the elites institutionalize injustice into what I have termed *force matrices*, in honor of the science fiction movie *The Matrix*, because these economic systems-of-control directly or indirectly siphon the people's production. Although the Financial Matrix is the elites' most powerful institutionalized injustice ever created, it has followed in the footsteps of earlier force matrices. In fact, there are three foundational force matrices, or systems-of-control used by the elites to capture the people's production. We can identify these by combining de Jouvenal's insight, that the elites seek to control human production, with the economic fact that there are only three factors of human production: labor, land, and capital.

Physical Matrix over Labor

The first is slavery, which we could coin the Physical Matrix, wherein the elites claim to own other people and thus monopolize their labor. The PRP for kings in ancient history, for example, manifested itself in the enslavement of people whom the kings claimed to *own*. Ancient monarchs would either monopolize the slaves' labor for profit or sell them to another elite who did so. It is a Physical Matrix because the elites claimed monopoly ownership, by force, over the physical person. This perverse force matrix therefore presumes to own the slave's labor (the first factor of production) because it *owns* the person. Perhaps the only positive about slavery is it was better than the alternative—the slaughtering of captives—which stopped when the elites realized slaves were more valuable alive than dead. If we traced our family trees back far enough, many of us would discover ancestors who suffered enslavement. Fortunately, by the end of the Roman Empire and with the growth of Christianity, slavery became economically and ethically unsupportable. This led to slavery falling out of favor in Europe during the Middle Ages. Regrettably, however, with the discovery of the New World, the Physical Matrix was reborn. The hunger for profit and the need for labor coalesced to somehow justify the unjustifiable, and Native Americans and Africans were enslaved by the English and American elites. La Rochefoucauld once said, "Hypocrisy is the tribute vice pays to virtue,"[6] and the rank hypocrisy of the Physical Matrix in America was a vice that stained America's ideals and reverberates to this day. The Physical Matrix, like all systems-of-control, is wrong, plain and simple.

Feudal Matrix over Land

During the early Middle Ages, the slavery of the Physical Matrix, for the most part, ended in Europe. The elites, however, driven by their Power Rule Philosophy, quickly moved to monopolize the ownership of land, the next factor of production. After all, the people needed land in order to farm, and thus, by controlling the land, the elites could control the people's production. This force matrix through the monopolization of land is known as serfdom, which we could call the Feudal Matrix. The elites claimed the right to control the land, forcing the people to pay a portion of their production for the privilege of using the landlord's property. Notice how the elites surrendered the claim that they owned the person but did not surrender control over the people. They merely shifted the control from the first factor of production (labor) to the second factor of production (land). In consequence, they still accomplished the same result—namely, the capture of the people's production. This was a less overt form of control because the serfs were technically free, but the profits still flowed to the elites through the Feudal Matrix. The elites, in other words, learned that indirectly capturing the masses' labor by monopolizing land was more profitable than directly capturing the labor through slavery. The Feudal Matrix generated more profits with less palpable control than the Physical Matrix. After all, it was borne out that people who can retain a portion of their productive efforts will work harder than slaves who retain none. This Feudal Matrix thrived until the revival of precious metal money in Europe, which made it possible for serfs to escape from the land of their overlords to the city where they could work for money. Butchers, bakers, and candlestick makers made products and exchanged them for money to purchase other products without needing their former landlords' land. The land monopoly force matrix, in consequence, collapsed, and the modern world was born.

Financial Matrix over Capital

Both the Physical Matrix (slavery) and the Feudal Matrix (serfdom) are taught widely in history class. But practically no one is aware of the existence of the third and most insidious of all: the Financial Matrix. This may be because it is still operational. Or perhaps its obscurity results from the elites more effectively concealing their plunder, as we'll see. The Financial

Matrix is, of course, the monopolization of capital, the third factor of production, which effectively makes people debt serfs or peons. Elites following the Power Rule Philosophy claimed monopoly ownership of the money supply in order to control people's production. Indeed, just as the Feudal Matrix monopolized the land to indirectly control the land serfs, so too does the Financial Matrix monopolize the money to indirectly control the debt peons.

In other words, whereas the Physical Matrix directly owned the person to control their labor, the Feudal and Financial Matrices achieved much better results by indirectly controlling *free* people. By monopolizing the other factors of production, the elites provided people the illusion of freedom while plundering their production. In fact, so long as debts and taxes are paid, the control is hardly noticed. However, when the debt serfs offend the financial lords by missing payments, punishment is meted out swiftly by exorbitant interest and the degradation of credit scores.

Elites following the Power Rule Philosophy have consistently captured the state's monopoly of force for *institutionalized injustice,* creating a force matrix over labor, land, or capital. As discussed, the Financial Matrix, through its worldwide monopoly over the money supply, captured state power to enforce its force matrix over the people. Now it is expanding its use of state power to rebuild versions of Feudal Matrix serfdom and Physical Matrix slavery. For instance, property owners must pay property taxes on *their* land or they lose it.

That is to say, property owners rent their land and are evicted if they stop payments. Governments, in consequence, have reinstituted the Feudal Matrix, since they are the effective monopoly owners of the land. Finally, even the Physical Matrix is making a comeback through the growing popularity of state socialism, an economic system wherein private property is abolished and the state owns and directs everything. In such wrongheaded systems, the state becomes the master and the people become *slaves,* with an effective tax rate of 100%, since as Marx said, they only receive compensation "according to their needs." [7]

Despite Herbert Spencer's warning that "socialism is slavery"[8] and the historical record of socialism as a series of economic collapses propped up by violence and force, pollster Frank Luntz recently discovered that 58% of what he called the "Snapchat generation" claim to prefer socialism to capitalism.[9]

To the younger generation's credit, they smell the dead economic rat, but the Media has blamed anything and everything for the rot except the true cause, the Financial Matrix FRB system. The Media has effectively divided the people into two camps. On one hand, the Media riles up the conservative right to support law, order, and family values. Believing they are defending the American values of liberty and justice, they are duped into supporting the Financial Matrix's oppression and injustice. On the other hand, the Media stirs up the liberal left to support change, charity, and equality.

Believing they are fighting against injustice and oppression, they are duped into protesting against the current economic system by promoting socialism— Physical Matrix slavery. In other words, the Media has so convoluted the economic issues that the two alternatives served to the people both result in Power Rule Philosophy plunder: they can be Financial Matrix debt serfs or Physical Matrix socialist slaves. This is a choice between remaining in the frying pan or jumping directly into the fire. In reality, the Physical Matrix socialist slavery is even worse than the Financial Matrix debt peons, as former Soviet Union economist Yuri Maltsev explained:

. . . in October 1917, Russia opened the most deadly experiment in human history, which resulted in the establishment of a regime of total public slavery. Destruction of market incentives led to the establishment of central planning, coercion, violence, and the subsequent mass murder of slaves. It was the only way to manage production and distribution under socialism. . . . Demographer Rudolph Rummel estimated the human toll of socialism to be about 61 million in the Soviet Union and roughly 200 million worldwide. These victims perished during government-organized famines, collectivizations, cultural revolutions, purges, campaigns against "unearned" income, and other devilish experiments in social engineering.[10]

For those who give credence to statements from leftist politicians who claim modern socialism has improved, consider the words of Marion Smith, the executive director of Victims of Communism:

Marxist ideology is still being used to hold more than a billion people captive around the globe. China, where Xi Jinping just proclaimed the Communist Manifesto's continued relevance, continues to use a system of Laogai, or forced labor camps, and dictates where the working class can live and work based on a "social credit" system. Venezuela's socialist regime seized the means of production. Venezuela's military runs the grocery stores while Nicolas Maduro denies humanitarian food aid to his political opponents. The average Venezuelan has lost more than 20 pounds in the last year.[11]

The Financial Matrix compared to the Physical Matrix may be the lesser of two evils, but why choose between two evils at all? People are left with false choices because the real solution, the Golden Rule Philosophy, is intentionally removed from public discussion. All that is allowed is bickering over which type of rope we'd like to hang ourselves with. Perhaps nothing displays the Media's obedience to the Financial Matrix more than its complete acquiescence to its Power Rule Philosophy plunder. Professor Allan Bloom observed:

> Freedom of the mind requires not only, or not even specially, the absence of legal constraints but the presence of alternative thoughts. The most successful tyranny is not the one that uses force to assure uniformity but the one that removes the awareness of other possibilities.[12]

The Media, in effect, has achieved this because it has removed the Golden Rule Philosophy from the discussion. And even when free enterprise is mentioned, the centrally controlled money by the Financial Matrix is assumed, an assumption that ensures the topic is anything but a truly free market.

Furthermore, the Media glosses over boom/bust economic failures caused by the FRB system. Instead, the people are persuaded by the Media to demand additional state regulations, leading to even more losses of freedoms. If we have learned anything from history, it is that the Power Rule Philosophy and the corresponding matrices enforced by the state were created to serve elites, not the people. Thus, for the people to live free, we must stop looking to the state for help and must instead do what historian Antony Sutton suggested:

The power system continues only as long as individuals try to get something for nothing. The day when a majority of individuals declares or acts as if it wants nothing from the government, declares that it will look after its own welfare and interests, then on that day the power elites are doomed. [13]

People can only act on what they know. What they know comes from what they've learned. And what they've learned comes from how they've been (or haven't been) educated. True education is the transmission of values, which is why all education is religious in nature.

The only question is whose values are being transmitted to the students, since to be morally neutral is impossible. Western civilization's education was founded on classic Greco-Roman literature, but combined with the transmission of Judeo-Christian Biblical absolute values. This formed the West's dynamic worldview, which, as it permeated society, allowed people to make moral judgments about past injustices to improve justice in the present.

The West transmitted Biblical values to help the people understand their rights and responsibilities to God, society, and self. Because people were made in God's image, they had the ability to think and reason. After all, a true education is not the regurgitation of facts, but learning how to think. Through asking questions, comparing and contrasting, and connecting ideas together in unique ways, thinking people innovatively solve challenges.

Sadly, the modern educational system is spending more money than ever while ensuring that people think less than ever. The modern education system is, regrettably, a modern indoctrination system, parroting approved doctrines to churn out waves of new adherents to the Financial Matrix system of control. Antony Sutton again pinpointed the main defect with modern education when he said it "stifles individual initiative and trains children to become mindless zombies, serving the State. We need a lot less propaganda for 'education' and a more individual creative search for learning. Instead of more money for education, we need to allocate a lot less. The existing system of education is little more than a conditioning mechanism. It has little to do with education in the true sense, and a lot to do with control of the individual."[13]

The good news is we now know the elite's playbook for building matrices to plunder people through labor, land, and capital. The oppressive matrices are relics from our barbaric past, whether an ancient king controlling captives from conquered cities, or aristocratic lords controlling land-serfs by monopolizing arable property, or today's financial elites controlling debt-serfs by monopolizing money; such systems-of-control are past their sell dates. It's time to throw these vulgar relics into the historical dustbin and relaunch civilization on the Golden Rule Philosophy, through which the people of the world can enjoy their God-given rights to life, liberty, and property under justice for all. This is the future, and as author Victor Hugo declared: "Nothing else in the world . . . not all the armies . . . is so powerful as an idea whose time has come."[14]

The Golden Rule Philosophy replaces matrices of control with free market production and restores the people's rights in the process. This can fire the dreams of people around the world by blowing oxygen on the embers of entrepreneurship currently suffocating under the Financial Matrix's absolute power.

The effort to free people from the grip of the Financial Matrix might accurately be called the Financial Justice Movement. It is led by a group of Rascals (to use my friend Chris Brady's term) entrepreneurs, who understand that people are born with God-given rights of life, liberty, and property and are responsible to develop their gifts in the pursuit of their dreams.

We understand these ideals will never be perfectly realized on Earth but nonetheless strive to provide liberty and justice for all. Anyone, no matter what race, creed, or ethnicity, who accepts responsibility will advance by serving others. These are the ideals that throughout history have inspired so many to resist tyranny and led Martin Luther King Jr. to proclaim, "I have a dream that my four little children will one day live in a nation where they will not be judged by the color of their skin but by the content of their character."[23] It's time to spread this idea throughout the world that free and responsible people, regardless of race, creed, or ethnicity, can enjoy their God-given rights and pursue their dreams under liberty and justice for all. This is an idea whose time has come.

The world would radically improve without the Financial Matrix because the true antithesis of the Power Rule Philosophy force matrix is the Golden Rule Philosophy free market. Whereas free market leadership is based on serving others, force matrix management, in contrast, is based on coercing others. Indeed, were society to replace the PRP Financial Matrix with the GRP Free Market, the people's standard of living would increase five times over! This is the total cost people pay the Financial Matrix because of taxes, monopolies, inflation, and debt. Furthermore, terminating the Financial Matrix would also end the fractional reserve banking system and its destructive boom/bust cycles.

Financial Justice requires economic freedom, which can only be achieved by ending the Financial Matrix and limiting state power. But it won't be easy. Albert Jay Nock said an unlimited state would never surrender:

This is one of many indications pointing to the great truth which apparently must forever remain unlearned, that if a régime of complete economic freedom be established, social and political freedom will follow automatically; and until it is established neither social nor political freedom can exist. Here one comes in sight of the reason why the State will never tolerate the establishment of economic freedom.[15]

The Golden Rule Philosophy is a system of beliefs, a worldview, that builds the framework for creating and living in a free society. Worldviews are vital for human action because actions are based on thoughts, which flow from a person's underlying philosophy of life. Indeed, what made Western civilization unique was the Golden Rule Philosophy that flowed from Biblical beliefs. Economist Edmund Opitz wrote:

The freedom quest of Western man, as it has exhibited itself periodically over the past 20 centuries, is not a characteristic of man as such. It is a cultural trait, philosophically and religiously inspired. The basic religious vision of the West regards the planet earth as the creation of a good God who gives a man a soul and makes him responsible for its proper ordering; puts him on earth as a sort of junior partner with dominion over the earth; admonishes him to be fruitful and multiply; commands him to work; makes him a steward of the earth's scarce resources; holds him accountable for their economic use; and makes theft wrong because property is right. When this outlook comes to prevail, the groundwork is laid for a free and prosperous commonwealth such as we aspired to on this continent.[16]

The Golden Rule Philosophy has nine distinct beliefs that, when interlinked together, form a worldview based on liberty and justice. And although no society has ever perfectly fulfilled these beliefs, practically every key advancement in the quality of life of humankind occurred during eras when this worldview was predominant. Europe decisively broke out of the civilizational pack in the early sixteenth century (not coincidentally, at the same time when the Bible was translated into the common languages of the people) and has enjoyed over five hundred years of compound growth while other civilizations remained basically stagnant.

For instance, in 1913 the total global economic output generated by Western civilization (societies founded on European heritage), with barely one-fifth of the world's population, was nearly four-fifths of the world's total. No other civilization accomplished so much for so long with so little, and this was a direct result of the improved liberty and justice the people enjoyed through the GRP. In practically every key measure of civilization, the West, as historian Niall Ferguson said, surpassed the rest. Unfortunately, since 1913 the West has been fading, and this is directly related to the growth of the Power Rule Philosophy Financial Matrix and the corresponding decline of the Golden Rule Philosophy.

Author David Boaz said those who claim to believe in the free market, "but advocate more and more confiscation of the wealth created by productive people, more and more restrictions on voluntary interaction, more and more exceptions to property rights and the rule of law, more and more transfer of power from society to state, are unwittingly engaged in the ultimately deadly undermining of civilization."[17] It's time to restore the Golden Rule Philosophy and shine the bright lights of liberty and justice for all upon the people of the world groping in oppressive darkness. The Golden Rule Philosophy, if one must put a label on it, would be Christian libertarianism, a laissez-faire (hands-off) political philosophy advocating only minimal state intervention in the lives of citizens. Christians believe in the Bible's moral absolutes and seek to live them in the world. With this ethical foundation, we can fruitfully study the secular libertarian economists. For example, libertarian economist David Boaz outlined nine key concepts of libertarianism.

The nine core beliefs are, in reality, Biblical beliefs, and when practiced with Biblical ethics, they produce the Golden Rule Philosophy. Indeed, the growth in Western civilization was the direct result of applying the Golden Rule Philosophy to the free market system.

1. Individualism

The GRP recognizes the individual as the basic unit of society. Each individual is responsible and accountable for his or her actions. Because human beings were made in the image of God, the GRP honors the dignity of the individual, who has rights and responsibilities within society because he or she has rights and responsibilities before God. This belief, over time, breaks down prejudices, since every human being is made in the image of God. This is one of the greatest victories for global freedom because every person has inherent human dignity and should have the same opportunity to advance, based upon his or her merits, as any other person.

2. Individual Rights

The Bible taught that men and women were accountable to an Almighty God; therefore, each individual is a moral agent, responsible to secure his or her life, liberty, and property. These rights were not given to the people by the government but are inherent within human nature. In fact, the proper charter for the government is to secure these individual rights by creating a common force to protect them all. Just as an individual does not have the right to transgress another individual's personal rights, neither does the government's common force have the right to transgress the individual's rights, because the individual had these rights before the government was formed.

3. Providential Order

Order is essential for society, and without it anarchy would quickly destroy all social arrangements. The GRP, however, explains that this order is not imposed upon society by a central authority, or spontaneously ordered as secular libertarians claim; rather, it is from the Creator. One of the greatest blessings to humanity is how out of the seemingly disparate actions of billions of people in the marketplace, order arises. The vital institutions that have made human society possible, including money, law, language, and the marketplace, are Providential gifts from an orderly God, developed without the need for central control. Civil society is merely the sum of all the individual purposes that, as Adam Smith noted, appear to be directed by an "invisible hand,"[18] creating order from perceived disorder. The truth is that a prosperous social order is created, not by controlling each individual's choices, but by setting them free. Social order derives from what at first blush appears to be disorder. The supply and demand for every product necessary for survival is coordinated through the self-acting price mechanism, and a Providential ordering of society results, based on who can best satisfy market demands. The price of each product signals entrepreneurs to either enter or exit the various markets, ensuring the most vital demands of the people are met. Not only is there no need for centralized control, but it is irrational to assume any human being would be capable of compiling the millions of data points necessary to centrally order the wholly decentralized free market system. Incidentally, this is the reason socialism is an economic disaster. Without a market price to balance supply and demand, the centralized controllers must set the prices for every product and service within society. And when prices are artificially set, the supply and demand levels are ensured to be hopelessly out of whack. Socialism always and everywhere leads to production shortages and long customer lines, resulting in the controllers resorting to coercion, force, and murder to keep people *enjoying the benefits*. Sure, ivory-tower college professors can sell socialistic dreams, but when theory meets economic reality, the dream turns into a nightmare. Once the controllers realize they do not have Godlike omniscience, they must apply an anti-Godlike force to make dissatisfied people comply.

4. The Rule of Law

Liberty does not give people the right to do anything they want without any consequences. Instead, liberty is married to justice to build a lawful society, in which people can freely pursue their dreams so long as they respect the liberty of others to pursue theirs. The important distinction to understand is that the rule of law means *the law is king,* as opposed to *the king is law.* The rule of law is vital for free individuals because it ensures they are not subject to the arbitrary whims of those in power. These laws set the boundaries of proper behavior and allow free individuals to pursue their dreams within those boundaries without economic or political interference. The more society is ruled by just laws, the more freedoms the people enjoy.

5. Limited Government

The main reason for eliminating the Financial Matrix is it is an absolute power, and as we have seen, absolute power is a supernova that draws much into itself before self-destructing. Without specific checks on power, including limited funding, the government quickly transforms into an absolute power with predictable tyrannical consequences. Ideally, individuals following the Golden Rule Principle establish limited governments that are mandated to safeguard justice and liberty. Anything a government does beyond this is a violation of its GRP charter. Written constitutions, as history has revealed, are not enough to restrain governments. Instead, the most effective check to ensure limited government is to limit the government's funding. Only when funds have been limited have governments truly been limited. This is why the Financial Matrix so easily captured state power. After all, with control of the central banking system, it provided for itself a source of unlimited funds. The history of Western civilization is one of the people struggling to remain free from the elites struggling to achieve absolute power.

6. The Virtue of Production

One of the strongest motives for immigrants to come to America in the nineteenth century was the dream to live free from the monarchs' and aristocrats' matrices-of-control. People have a God-given right to enjoy the benefits of their own labor without it being siphoned off by the elites in power. Whereas the ancient Greeks and Romans believed manual labor was beneath their dignity and only fit for slaves, the Biblical perspective considered work as a calling and not below anyone. In fact, if people use their liberty not to work, then they will suffer, as the Apostle Paul once said: "He who will not work, will not eat."[19]

The matrices-of-control, therefore, are unjust because elites should not remain idle by unjustly siphoning from the production of others. Thomas Paine writing about European countries said, "There are two distinct classes of men in the nation, those who pay taxes, and those who receive and live upon the taxes."[20] This is why so many people braved the Atlantic crossing to escape to the New World. Unfortunately, the matrices-of-control eventually followed them, and now the new has become like the old. Alas, there are now no new continents to escape to, so the people must revive the Golden Rule Philosophy and end the matrices-of-control once and for all.

7. Natural Harmony of Interests

There is a natural harmony of interests under justice and liberty wherein peaceful and productive people can prosper through free exchanges. Although there is competition within society, the competition among firms creates cooperation within each firm as they seek to compete to satisfy customers. Sure, individual plans can be thwarted (for instance, another person hired for work or outbids you for a house or even outcourts you for a spouse), but the overall effect is to ensure free people make free choices. This *harmony of interest* ensures the people who best serve their customers prosper while those who don't either change their approach or move to a field more suited to their talents. Under a GRP Free Market, there is no conflict among farmers, manufacturers, marketers, entrepreneurs, and employees. The tide rises and falls for all of them based on producing products that serve customers. Only under matrices-of-control, where the government gives special deals to a few at the expense of the many, does the system become unbalanced and the harmony of interest break down.

8. Peace

The Golden Rule Philosophy is completely against offensive war. After all, if we do unto others as we would have them do unto us, I doubt any of us would want someone to enter our house and take all our belongings. Much worse, war is entering another country and violently taking life, limb, and property. War not only brings death and destruction, but does so at great financial and social costs. War greatly increases taxes, expenses, and centralization as the state strives for absolute power in an all-out effort to defeat its enemy. Nothing is more harmful to the welfare of the people while shamefully beneficial to the ruling elites as warfare. A nation's military is supposed to be for defense, not offense. However, when a state receives unlimited funding, it quickly achieves absolute power, turning from the legitimate use of the military to protect its citizens to illegitimately bullying weaker nations. And any power strong enough to bully other nations soon realizes it is strong enough to bully its own people as well. War is the greatest scourge of liberty and justice known to humankind, and despite all the state's justifications, to force unwilling draftees to fight in foreign wars against their wishes is not a legitimate role of the state, for it violates the draftees' right to life and liberty. This is why throughout history, war has usually been the enemy of peaceful and productive people on both sides of every conflict.

9. Free Markets

It's vital to understand that the free market system is the natural result of applying the Biblical worldview to economics. After all, three of the Ten Commandments—"Thou shall not kill," "Thou shall not steal," and 'Thou shall not covet"—emphasize the importance of respecting people's God-given rights to life, liberty, and property. When this is combined with the inherent dignity of being created by God in His image, we see why the free market system treats people as morally responsible agents, who have the liberty to build their lives and property as they see fit, so long as they respect the God-given rights of others. The GRP was not created in a vacuum. Because of the sixteenth-century invention of the printing press and Biblical translations into common languages, European society transformed from most churches not owning a Bible to many commoners owning and reading them in their own homes. As a result, the sixteenth century, not coincidentally, was also when the free market system exploded onto the scene. The Bible emphasizes our ethical accountability to an Almighty God, teaching that human beings are created for liberty (2 Corinthians 3:17: "where the Spirit of the Lord is, there is liberty") and justice (Micah 6:8: "what does the Lord require of you but to do justice, and to love kindness, and to walk humbly"). Altogether, the Biblical worldview connected the spiritual, economic, and political spheres because the Bible revealed that God's law reigned in all areas, "on earth as it is in heaven."

The Golden Rule Philosophy declares that government should be limited to maintaining justice before the law for everyone and otherwise keep its hands off life, liberty, and property. Free markets provide an environment for production without plunder, while the matrices-of-control provide the elites with plunder without production. When the state is allowed to be economically sovereign over consumers, the people live in a force matrix and are not free. However, when the free market allows consumers to be economically sovereign over their property, the people live free, as economist Ludwig von Mises explained:

> The real bosses [under free markets] are the
> consumers. They, by their buying and by their abstention
> from buying, decide who should own the capital and run
> the plants. They determine what should be produced and
> in what quantity and quality. Their attitudes result either
> in profit or in loss for the enterpriser. They make poor
> men rich and rich men poor. They are no easy bosses.
> They are full of whims and fancies, changeable and
> unpredictable. They do not care a whit for past merit.
> As soon as something is offered to them that they like
> better or is cheaper, they desert their old purveyors.[21]

The GRP Free Market system is fair, just, and equitable. So
why has the unfair, unjust, and inequitable PRP matrices-of-control prospered in the twentieth century and beyond? Author Edmund Opitz provides the key insight: "A man may live according
to his father's code even after abandoning the faith which gave
the father his code. But the grandson will have neither faith,
nor code."[22] In other words, faith and ethics are connected, and
when one is lost, the other is sure to follow. Unfortunately, just
as a fish is the last one to discover water, most secular economists miss the vital connection between the free market and
its Biblical ethics foundation. Modern libertarianism believed it
could secularize the free market system by denying its Biblical
framework. But as Opitz clearly explained, when society loses its
faith in the Biblical God, within a generation or two, the Biblical
ethics vanishes as well. And without its Biblical foundation, the
free market is rudderless, lost at sea.

When the people deny ethical absolutes, they are unable to
defend themselves against injustices, for according to the relativistic worldview, there is no right and wrong. Martin Luther King
Jr. depicted what this Godless philosophy, which might sound

just fine in the college classroom, actually looks like in the lives
of real people when he said:

> Any religion that professes to be concerned about
> the souls of men and is not concerned about the slums
> that damn them, the economic conditions that strangle
> them and the social conditions that cripple them is a
> spiritually moribund religion awaiting burial.[23]

This is the purpose of this book. The disastrous result of
our educational system's disregard of moral absolutes in favor
of relativistic nonsense is that the people are then sentenced to
financial injustice. C. S. Lewis warned of the dangers of moral
relativism during the second World War when he wrote:

> In a sort of ghastly simplicity we remove the organ
> and demand the function. We make men without chests
> and expect of them virtue and enterprise. We laugh at
> honour and are shocked to find traitors in our midst. We
> castrate and bid the geldings be fruitful.[24]

Fortunately, the truth sets people free. And despite our current educational system's attempt to bury it, the truth of the
Biblical worldview is the soul of Western civilization. For over a
thousand years, the Bible fueled the West's spiritual, economic,
and political growth because, as author Vishal Mangalwadi said:

> . . . it propelled the development of everything
> good in the West: its notion of human dignity, human
> rights, human equality, justice, optimism, heroism,
> rationality, family, education, universities, technology,

science, culture of compassion, great literature, heroism, economic progress, political freedom.[25]

Disastrously, however, in the twenty-first century, as Manga-lwadi observed, "The West has amputated its soul."[25] Naturally, without the soul, Western civilization is a comatose body without purpose, meaning, and direction. Without absolute truths, the people have invited elites to plunder them, and we should not be surprised that they accepted the invitation. Fortunately, just as the failure of the Golden Rule Philosophy began with the loss of Biblical absolutes and obedience to the state's absolute sovereignty, the revival of the free market system begins with the restoration of our God-given rights to life, liberty, and property and obedience to God's absolute sovereignty.

A society that puts equality before freedom will get neither, a society that puts freedom before equality will get a high degree of both.

—Milton Friedman

CHAPTER 6

Declaration of Independence: Freedom over Force

Throughout history, human society has been structured around force or freedom, as my friend George Guzzardo has so eloquently expressed in his book *Torch of Freedom*.[1] When force matrices become too oppressive, people seek to escape their reach. For example, near the end of the Roman Empire, taxes became so oppressive that citizens escaped their reach by living with the barbarians. Similarly, near the end of the Medieval age, serfs moved to cities to escape the oppressive reach of their landlords. For the last five hundred years, people have sought to escape the force matrices by coming to America, the land of freedom. Unfortunately, the Financial Matrix has now captured the world, and there is no place to move where it isn't in control. Imagine, however, if there were a way to escape it, not by moving to faraway lands, but simply by unplugging from the money and banking system controlled by the Financial Matrix. Imagine a community committed to restoring Financial Justice worldwide through practicing the Golden Rule Philosophy and utilizing the free market system. Imagine a movement supported by a business platform through which customers can enjoy numerous benefits and entrepreneurs are rewarded for spreading the message. The good news is that such a movement doesn't have to be imagined; it already exists.

People will either continue to be oppressed within the PRP force matrices, or will unite to build a just GRP Free Market. Force or freedom are the only two choices. This has been the story throughout history, with elites seeking control through force matrices and people seeking freedom through free markets. Consider the scene from the movie *Braveheart* in which William Wallace rouses his troops, which speaks to this age-old urge for freedom from control:

> William Wallace: I am William Wallace. And I see a whole army of my countrymen, here in defiance of tyranny! You have come to fight as free men. And free men you are! What will you do with that freedom? Will you fight?!

> Young Soldier: No, we will run and live!

> William Wallace: Yes! Fight and you may die. Run and you will live at least awhile. And dying in your bed many years from now, would you be willing to trade all the days from this day to that for one chance, just one chance, to come back here as young men and tell our enemies that they may take our lives but they will never take our freedom!!! [2]

William Wallace was a leader who inspired people to unite to fight for their freedoms. By contrast, the aristocratic Robert the Bruce recognized that coercion could never inspire in a similar fashion. From the same movie:

Robert the Bruce: I have nothing. Men fight for me because if they do not, I throw them off my land and I starve their wives and their children. Those men who bled the ground red at Falkirk, they fought for William Wallace, and he fights for something that I never had. And I took it from him, when I betrayed him. I saw it in his face on the battlefield and it's tearing me apart.

Robert the Bruce's father: All men betray. All lose heart.

Robert the Bruce: I don't wanna lose heart. I wanna believe as he does.[2]

A similar passion is what drove Thomas Jefferson to pen one of the greatest odes to freedom ever written: the American Declaration of Independence. In 1776, Jefferson captured the self-evident (Biblical) principles that have motivated many people for many years to escape tyranny and live free. And despite hardships and hypocrisies, that document's ideals still speak to us today. One of the most impactful paragraphs states:

We hold these truths to be self-evident, that all men are created equal, that they are endowed by their Creator with certain unalienable Rights, that among these are Life, Liberty and the pursuit of Happiness. That to secure these rights, Governments are instituted among Men, deriving their just powers from the consent of the governed, That whenever any Form of Government becomes destructive of these ends, it is the Right of the People to alter or to abolish it, and to institute new Government, laying its foundation on such principles

and organizing its powers in such form, as to them shall
seem most likely to effect their Safety and Happiness.

Unfortunately, as with all noble ideals, the Founders discovered it was much easier to profess free market principles than to
live them. After all, for nearly a century after that declaration,
Physical Matrix slavery was still routinely practiced in America.
Nonetheless, self-evident truths do not die easily, and Martin
Luther King Jr. used these very principles to expose the gap between America's rhetoric and its reality. He challenged all of us
to live up to our noble founding ideals, emphasizing that when
we do not protect the God-given rights of others, we imperil
our own. For instance, if a foreign state attempted to conquer
and enslave our society, we would rise up to defend ourselves.
Now that we know the Financial Matrix has captured the state
and is unjustly ruling with the Power Rule Philosophy, a similar
response to protect ourselves is warranted. Should we bow in
craven fear and accept our financial enslavement, or will we, like
Patrick Henry, proclaim:

> Why stand we here idle? What is it that gentlemen
> wish? What would they have? Is life so dear, or peace
> so sweet, as to be purchased at the price of chains and
> slavery? Forbid it, Almighty God! I know not what
> course others may take; but as for me, give me liberty
> or give me death! [3]

No one is coerced into freedom; rather, it is earned by free
people behaving responsibly. It's time to reclaim our God-given
rights, restore the free market system, and return Financial Justice to oppressed people worldwide. King also said, "In the end,
we will remember not the words of our enemies, but the silence

of our friends."[4] We cannot remain silent in the face of rank injustice. This book exposes the Financial Matrix, and just as our ancestors sought to escape the Physical and Feudal Matrices, it's time for us to declare our independence from the Financial Matrix, and its oppressive money and banking system. People are drowning in financial tyranny, made more dangerous by the fact that many still don't realize it, and it's time someone builds an escape route to help set them free. To do so, we must end the Power Rule Philosophy force matrices and replace them with the Golden Rule Philosophy Free Market.

Interestingly, while the GRP is only possible in a free market system, the PRP is possible in any number of force matrices using the three factors of production (labor, land, and capital). Author Leo Tolstoy once wrote: "Happy families are all alike; every unhappy family is unhappy in its own way."[5] Similarly, every GRP economy is alike (implementing the free market), but every PRP economy is unjust in its own way (implementing any number of force matrix variations). F. A. Hayek's "road to serfdom"[6] has many lanes, but there is only one road to liberty and justice, and that is the GRP Free Market. We must decide whether we wish to live under PRP force or escape to GRP freedom, because we cannot have both. And since the Media has done such an effective job selling us on our own enslavement, we must take the time to separate fact from fiction when comparing force matrices and free markets. After all, the Financial Matrix has invested trillions of dollars obfuscating the issues in order to ensure its rule.

Again, there are only two basic economic systems: force matrices or free markets. Whether the force matrix is Physical, Feudal, or Financial in nature, the outcome is economic tyranny because the people are treated as slaves and serfs whose production the elites plunder. However, when we declare our independence from force matrices, the free market is the natural result. Although no society has ever freed itself entirely from force matrices, every move toward greater economic freedom has led to an explosion in prosperity.

One of the best case studies that exhibits the difference between force matrix and free market results is post–World War II Germany. During the war, Hitler had instituted food rations, limiting its civilian population to no more than two thousand calories per day. After the war, the Allies inherited an economic mess. Between continued food-rationing policies, price controls, and massive inflation, the only part of the German economy that was thriving was the black market. Germany was occupied after the war and soon divided in half, with the eastern half forced into the socialist policies of the Soviet Union and the western half following the more free-market-oriented policies of America. The two Germanys, with the same culture and language, and having experienced a total economic reset, would now attempt to rebuild using competing economic systems. Not surprisingly, the free market blew away the force matrix.

Economist Ludwig Erhard played a vital role. He formulated the free market initiatives that revived West Germany's debilitated economy. First, he encouraged the Allies to issue a new currency to replace the worthless German currency. This plan squashed the runaway inflation, reducing the currency available to the public by a staggering 93%. Furthermore, he insisted on large tax cuts to spur private investment and spending. On June 21, 1948, the new currency was scheduled to be introduced, but Erhard still had one more ace up his sleeve. In an almost universally criticized move, Erhard freed the marketplace by removing all price controls.

Even the Americans, who were by then dabbling with Keynesian mixed economy policies (a combination of free markets and force matrices), vehemently disagreed. In fact, American General Lucius Clay, who was the military head of occupied West Germany, told Erhard that his advisers believed the new policies were a mistake. Undaunted, Erhard responded, "Don't listen to them, General. My advisers tell me the same thing." Erhard had made West Germany more of a free market, temporarily, than the American occupiers' economy. And the rest, as they say, is history. As the chart reveals, West Germany's free market economy more than doubled the productivity of East Germany's force matrix (socialist) economy.[7]

Economic output, however, doesn't tell the whole story. The Germans are some of the most car-loving people in the world, and their autobahn is legendary for having no posted speed limits. And it is in the area of automobiles that the true colors of the two systems are revealed. In a country artificially split between the Soviet socialist side (the east) and a free market one (the west), a unique comparison was presented to the world when the *Iron Curtain* was lifted in 1989.

At that time, the BMW 3 Series sedan, engineered and produced in West Germany, was one of the most popular and technologically sophisticated cars in the world, featuring fuel injection, antilock brakes, electronic controls of all sorts, traction control, and an exhaustive list of automotive innovation. In laughable contrast, from East Germany came the Trabant, a hopelessly underpowered two-stroke (!) car made from recycled waste with no tachometer, turn signals, seat belts, or even a fuel gauge.

This little beauty topped out at a whopping sixty miles per hour, but took twenty-one seconds to get there. What's more, there was a ten-year waiting list for any lucky would-be purchaser. No matter the type of intellectual clothing elite educators and peddlers of socialist principles use to dress up their ideas, they are never anything more than rotting skeletons underneath. After all, the bankruptcy of socialism could never have a better poster child than the hapless Trabant.

Now that we have seen how force matrix systems fail, let's study how the free market succeeds. The free market system is supported by six freedom pillars, pillars which every force matrix economic system violates. To display the difference, let's study each of the pillars to see how the free market system follows and the Financial Matrix violates them. The six pillars supporting the free market are: 1) consumer sovereignty, 2) private property, 3) free competition, 4) voluntary exchange, 5) price system, and 6) entrepreneurship.

Consumer Sovereignty

In a free market economy, the customer is sovereign. Customers get to enjoy economic liberty to select the products and services they want, so long as they do not violate the life, liberty, and property of others. Free markets are an economic democracy, wherein each consumer bids (votes) with their money to purchase goods and services in the marketplace. These economic bids, in turn, balance the supply of the economic item to the demand. The producer sets the price at which they believe the quantity produced can be sold for a profit.

In setting this price, the producer must consider what consumers will likely spend on the product, the prices of competitive products, and the cost of production. And even though producers set the price, under a free market system the consumers are the final decision makers because they can choose to buy or abstain from buying at that price. The market price of each economic good, in consequence, sells the total supply because it is the lowest price that the most aggressive seller will accept and it's the highest bid the most passive buyer will bid.

By contrast, the statist force matrix economy controls the customers and producers by capturing the land, labor, or capital of a society. They do so to dictate higher prices to consumers and higher profits for themselves. For instance, the Financial Matrix that we live under today has monopolized the money supply, and since it is legally allowed to create money out of thin air, it sets an artificially low price (the interest rate) for money, which is why total debts have exploded. In addition, through the state's legal tender laws, it mandates the acceptance of fiat paper money, forbidding consumers from working around this fake money by demanding precious metal money or something like cryptocurrency instead.

Consumers, as a result, are not monetarily free because they must use the state's fiat money and are not free to compete against the state-supported banking cartel. The Financial Matrix is sovereign over money matters, and the customers must obey. This is the antithesis of free markets, and therefore of liberty and justice for all.

Right to Private Property

Private property is foundational to free markets and ensures one of the people's natural rights to own their life, liberty, and property. Private property is the ownership of land, homes, cars, precious metals, and all other assets by individuals, families, or groups. Public property is owned by governments, such as the city hall, a park, or a highway, used to serve the public. Private property ownership leads directly to the division of labor, as people specialize in specific fields and then use money earned from that specialization to exchange for one another's goods and services. Free and responsible people making free choices of what to do with their property extend the division of labor and market wider and wider as more people choose to participate in the free market production and exchange system. In a free market, the people's right to buy and sell private property is guaranteed by a limited government protecting life, liberty, and property.

Under statism, however, an all-powerful state (like the East Germany example) owns and controls all property, and the people are allowed to use this public property only at the state's discretion. The Financial Matrix violates private property in several ways. Originally, fractional reserve banking robbed the value of the owners of precious metal money by fraudulently creating more metaphysical titles than existing precious metal money. This inflation of the money supply, as explained earlier, is property theft through debasing the purchasing power (value) of the owner's money. Second, the Financial Matrix directs the state to create property taxes on all private properties, causing all property, in a sense, to be rented from the State. If this rent is not paid, then the State reclaims the *owner's* land. Additionally, there is eminent domain, the right of a government to expropriate private property for public use for a token price, regardless of whether or not the *owners* approve. Private property, in other words, is no longer private, but is becoming progressively owned by the state, and obedient people are permitted to use it.

Free Competition

Competition is possible only where there are no restrictions for potential competitors to enter and exit the marketplace. Free market competition ensures the best businesses and employees are rewarded, because the customers vote for them with their money. After all, if entrepreneurs and businesses cannot satisfy customers, those customers are free to seek other competitors to serve them. The free market ensures business rivals seek the best leaders, the best employees, and the best strategies toward satisfying customers. Competition rewards successful businesses with profits and punishes unsuccessful ones with losses, based on free customers voting with their money. True competition externally creates true cooperation internally as businesses realize they must satisfy customers better than the competition in order to survive. As Peter Senge once said, "The only sustainable competitive advantage is your organization's ability to learn faster than the competition."[8] Free competition protects customer sovereignty because when not happy, they will look for who does make them happy.

Statism, however, creates monopolies by prohibiting potential competitors from entering the marketplace. This ensures higher profits for monopolies for less effort. Of course, this windfall comes at the customer's expense, because they pay higher prices and have fewer choices and benefits. Monopolists desire to be the only dog in the fight, ensuring they take home all the prizes regardless of actual performance. State monopolies and cartels are not competitive because the state restricts competition through overbearing regulations that squash all possible competition. And since there is little competition, there is little fear of losing customers, and thus little innovation (as in the Trabant example). Without competition, as economist Joseph Schumpeter noted, there is little creative destruction, the constant improvement that makes old practices obsolete. This is because companies are not worried about losing customers since they do not have any competitors. Not surprisingly, the more the force matrix operates within the economy, the less creative destruction occurs, and the economy stagnates without innovation.

The Financial Matrix violates the competition pillar because it does not allow competition at all. The fractional reserve banks cooperate with the central banks in the highly regulated financial field. In fact, it is against the law for outsiders to enter the banking field and innovate because they must comply with the onerous regulations that ensure bureaucratic obedience. Until free market competition is allowed in the banking system, the Financial Matrix will continue to oppress, and innovation will be repressed worldwide. This is why restoring competition within the banking sector would do more to advance the GRP Free Market system than practically anything else.

Voluntary Exchange

Free market transactions are voluntary and noncoercive because force cannot be used to coerce people into exchanges they do not desire. Free market trades benefit both sides or they are not completed. As such, if people believe a business or employer is mistreating them, the free market allows them to voluntarily withdraw to find a more satisfactory arrangement. The key to voluntary exchanges is the principle of win-win, for win-lose cannot be completed without coercion. By contrast, force matrix transactions are controlled through force or the law's threat of force.

Not surprisingly, the Financial Matrix is win-lose because it forces everyone to use fiat money by law. This forced restriction upon the people, that they must use one and only one money for their transactions, represents a trampling of freedom by shattering the Free Exchange pillar. Despite fiat money being created out of thin air and consistently losing purchasing power, the state's legal-tender laws mandate Federal Reserve banknotes (what most call US dollars) must be accepted. In fact, a person who refuses to accept fiat money has broken the law and will suffer legal consequences. Money, in short, is not a voluntary exchange, which confirms that the Financial Matrix has used the state's force to break this pillar.

The Price System

Prices for each good and service are produced by the voluntary exchange bidding process, through which the quantity of supply and the level of demand are balanced. Freedom in transactions produces a self-regulating free market price between the supply and demand for each product and service. In a free market, the government is laissez-faire, or *hands off*, meaning they do not allocate or dictate supply or prices to private organizations. Further, under free markets, the government does not dictate how goods and services are distributed. This, again, is properly done through voluntary trades in the marketplace. The price of each product is essential because entrepreneurs use the price signal (tracking price movements) to determine which items are in demand and where profits are possible. Indeed, without the free market price system, the entrepreneur would be blind, unable to make rational decisions for where to invest their time, money, and resources.

Price controls of any type are a direct violation of the Price System pillar, for it is a state intervention into the self-regulating price system. The Financial Matrix, instead of allowing the supply (money from savers) and demand (borrowers) to set the price of money (interest rates), artificially sets the price for money in the same way the socialist's system artificially sets the price for everything else. This is economic schizophrenia, for it proposes to run the money supply on socialist theory while proclaiming free markets for everything else. Because the supply, demand, and resulting price are the heartbeat of the free market system, an artificial interest rate, combined with the fractional reserve banking system, creates the boom/bust cycle, which is like a heart attack. This is because it destabilizes the heartbeat signals through its inflationary and deflationary processes. The Federal Reserve is monetary socialism.

Free Entrepreneurship

True entrepreneurs are innovative leaders, the catalyst for increases in supply, quality, and variety in the marketplace. The economy thrives when entrepreneurs are allowed to compete, innovate, and profit when successfully satisfying customers. Since an economy stagnates without entrepreneurs, the most prosperous societies know to provide the economic and legal framework to ensure entrepreneurs who invest capital to better serve customers are rewarded with profit when they do. What is termed the Austrian School of Economics was the first to recognize the importance of entrepreneurship to a properly working free market system. Critically, they observed that entrepreneurs are those bold souls who discover market disequilibrium, the gap between what customers want and what is currently available, and then fill it. These entrepreneurs capitalize on this disequilibrium by innovating in order to lower prices and provide better products for customers, while creating profits for themselves.

In force matrices, entrepreneurs are replaced with state bureaucrats, who decide what is important and what is not by the price they artificially set for each item. Perhaps, more than anything else, the elimination of entrepreneurial rewards has been the biggest cause of force matrix economic failures. Growth requires innovation, which requires rewarding entrepreneurs who innovate to satisfy customers. Regrettably, the Financial Matrix has caused one of the greatest disequilibriums in the world economy—namely, the fractional reserve banking system.

Entrepreneurs are not allowed to enter the monetary sector and creatively destroy the bad practices hindering the modern economy. Instead, the Financial Matrix has used state force to block innovation in that arena through its oppressive regulations and legal tender laws. Ironically, the same entrepreneurs who could fix the monetary instability are the ones suffering the most from the boom/bust cycles discombobulating the price mechanism. Entrepreneurship is challenging enough with proper price signals, but when interest rate prices for money are set by state-protected central banks, the supply and demand for money becomes imbalanced.

Predictably, during the 2008 financial crisis, it was the false price signals that bankrupted entrepreneurs en masse. In reality, the entrepreneurs did not fail, but the Financial Matrix failed them, resulting in a systemic boom/bust collapse. Until entrepreneurs are allowed to creatively destroy the unconscionable FRB system, the Financial Matrix will continue its monopoly of power and profits over the people.

Everywhere the six pillars have been respected and applied, prosperity has followed. This is our worldwide objective—namely, to rebuild the Golden Rule Philosophy foundation and restore the six pillars of the free market system. In the process, the hegemony of the Power Rule Philosophy Financial Matrix will be terminated. As stated previously, although it is no longer possible to escape the Financial Matrix by moving to faraway lands, people can still fight back against the Financial Matrix by following Buckminster Fuller's advice mentioned in the prologue: "You never change things by fighting the existing reality. In order to change something, you need to build a new model that makes the existing one obsolete."[9] Indeed, Fuller's viewpoint and a discussion with my great friend and CEO of Life, Chris Brady, led to our breakthrough business platform, which delivers nothing less than a way to make the Financial Matrix obsolete.

Inspired by Simon Sinek's book *Start with Why*,[10] we concluded that most entrepreneurs build businesses for profit, some build businesses on purpose, but only the greatest entrepreneurs build their purpose on a business. And after twenty-five years in the leadership genre, including writing multiple *New York Times* best sellers, setting a Guinness World Record, and speaking in front of hundreds of thousands of entrepreneurs globally, we built our business with a purpose to lead people to truth that made a difference in their lives.

However, through endless hours of research into the financial system and speaking personally to thousands of individuals attending our leadership events worldwide, while seeing inflation, debt, and tax levels rising precipitously, we came to the realization that leadership alone was not enough. This is because of the undeniable fact, as we've shown, that the financial system is rigged against the individual.

With compound debt outrunning most people's ability to compound earnings, the dream for a better life has drifted out of reach for many. Building our purpose on a business, we intend to bring Financial Justice to people, not by fighting against the Financial Matrix, but by minimizing its deleterious effects on individuals through offering them a product we call the Super App platform. We are, in effect, restoring Financial Justice with every Super App subscriber who learns how to escape the Financial Matrix. We will provide more detail in the next chapter on how exactly this breakthrough product can accomplish so much, but for now let's stay focused on why we developed what we did.

Sinek's book examined what motivated customers to buy from specific brands and discovered the key was how they marketed themselves. His breakthrough insight was "The Golden Circle," a diagram that explains the three subliminal questions consumers ask and answer during the purchasing process: the why, how, and what.[10] Sinek explained that the difference between the performance of different brands was the order in which these three questions were presented.

Most brands start from the outside and then work in, explaining what they do, followed by how they do it. But they miss the most important aspect—namely, why do they do what they do? The Golden Circle captures how iconic brands such as Apple and Harley-Davidson answer these questions in the reverse order of traditional marketers, answering *why* they exist before explaining the *what* and the *how*.

The Golden Circle

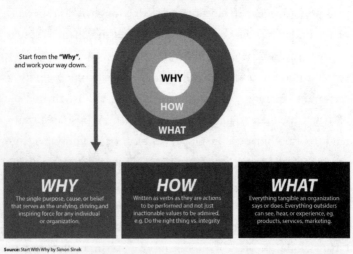

Start from the **"Why"**, and work your way down.

WHY
HOW
WHAT

WHY
The single purpose, cause, or belief that serves as the unifying, driving and inspiring force for any individual or organization.

HOW
Written as verbs as they are actions to be performed and not just inactionable values to be admired. e.g. Do the right thing vs. integrity

WHAT
Everything tangible an organization says or does. Everything outsiders can see, hear, or experience, e.g. products, services, marketing.

Source: Start With Why by Simon Sinek

Life's *why* is to set people free from the Financial Matrix. *How* we do this is through building communities to restore Financial Justice. As our community of loyal customers and members grows, more people are exposed to the oppressive nature of the Financial Matrix system and what they can do about it. Finally, *what* we do is leverage a Super App that empowers the escape from the Financial Matrix. We believe everyone should enjoy executive-level benefits for being part of the Financial Justice movement as they Have Fun, Make Money, and Make a Difference by using Life's Super App platform. Just like other successful brands, people use the Super App for more than just receiving immense value; they also use it because they support economic freedom over force and know by using the Super App that they are taking a bite out of the Financial Matrix. Every customer plays a part in the Financial Justice movement as he or she learns and shares the truth about the Financial Matrix. In this way, the message moves our product, and the product advances the message.

Life's Golden Circle

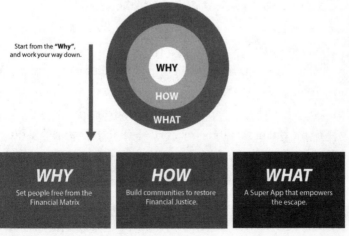

Start from the **"Why"**, and work your way down.

WHY	HOW	WHAT
Set people free from the Financial Matrix	Build communities to restore Financial Justice.	A Super App that empowers the escape.

Source: Start With Why by Simon Sinek

The best brands do not have mere customers; instead, they have a community of believers. Consider the rabid fans of Apple or Harley-Davidson. These are customers who support the brand not only for the value of their products, but also because they buy into the movement behind the brand and want to play a part in turning the *why* into reality. Whereas run-of-the-mill customers study function, features, and price in order to benefit themselves, a community of believers instead begins with the end in mind, aligning with how the movement makes the world better.

Nature recently provided me with an unforgettable illustration of a critical difference between mere customers and loyal community members. The lakeshore near our house was overrun with a gaggle of geese. Although we have previously had hundreds of geese drop by for a night or two, we never had any geese choose to stay for the summer. Perhaps, as my wife Laurie humorously suggested, these Canadian geese were turned back at the border due to COVID-19. After all, it was the summer of 2020, and anything was possible. The geese had requisitioned our grassy area in front of our pavilion and dock and had proceeded to make a mess of the place. After several weeks of our dog driving them into the water only to find they'd returned to the comfortable grass as soon as he left, I realized we had a problem. With several parties planned for later that summer, it would be difficult to enjoy a day at the lake if our guests were forced to trudge through inch-deep goose droppings.

Some online sleuthing revealed several ways to safely drive off unwanted geese. One simple solution involved attaching kite string to wooden planks about a foot off the ground at the point where the geese swim to shore. The idea seemed preposterous. First of all, the geese are sizable enough to just push right through the strings, upending the stakes, and eliminating the would-be defense. Second, geese can fly, and it would be no big deal to flap into the air for a few feet. I almost called off the whole foolish experiment on the basis of it most likely being a prank.

After all, Canadian geese routinely fly 1,500 miles per day in all kinds of weather conditions while traversing North America every year. How would a foot-high kite string make any difference? Nevertheless, we were desperate and decided to at least give it a try. The next morning, Laurie and I were shocked to see that half the geese were gone and the other half were walking around the parking area looking perplexed. No geese at all were on the grass or dock area where they had previously hung out. Although I wasn't convinced yet, I certainly was encouraged enough to keep the string in place for another day.

Amazingly, the next morning the geese were entirely gone. At the time of this writing, it's been several months and none of them have returned. Sure, we still have the occasional group of geese visit the lake as before, but none have attempted to come up to the grass because of the "highly inconvenient"c foot-high kite string.

The geese and the string present a wonderful analogy of the difference between regular customers and community members. Whereas normal customers, like the first group of geese, are driven off by the slightest inconvenience, a community of brand-believing customers will stick around longer because they believe in the *why* behind the product, hoping the inconvenience will be corrected. Entrepreneurs, going further, realize they can easily jump over the rope and will do so for as long as necessary.

After all, there is no such thing as entrepreneurship without strings. The geese can easily fly over the string, but normal customers won't because they are focused only on their convenience, whereas brand believers do inconvenience themselves, and entrepreneurs routinely sacrifice to turn the vision into reality. In other words, Super App community members are more loyal than typical customers because they believe in Financial Justice, the movement behind the Super App; however, entrepreneurs are sticky to a whole new level and, unlike the geese, will not seek another home when business gets inconvenient because they know they are paid to jump over strings.

The fact that you have read this far tells me that you are not a normal customer, for unlike the geese, you have inconvenienced yourself, investing your time to learn why we do what we do. The next chapter will discuss the Super App and the role community members and entrepreneurs can play in helping restore Financial Justice by having fun, making money, and making a difference.

If we tried to think of a good idea, we wouldn't have been able to think of a good idea. You just have to find the solution for a problem in your own life.

—Brian Chesky, Cofounder of Airbnb

CHAPTER 7

Financial Justice: The Super App Solution

For over twenty-five years, Chris Brady and I have been business partners. He is the one who conceptualized and led the development of the Super App. Brady is recognized as one of *Inc. Magazine's* Top 50 Leaders, a *New York Times* best-selling author, and the CEO of Life. The Super App platform enables people to Have Fun, Make Money, and Make a Difference and escape the Financial Matrix. Following the advice of Charles Schwab— 'Success all comes down to customer demand. Build something you would want to use yourself and recommend to your mother."[1]—Brady and his team created just such a product customers love. Moreover, customers of the Super App are supporting the Financial Justice movement, proclaiming like Patrick Henry and Martin Luther King Jr. that they prefer economic freedom over force. Altogether, customers enjoy an overwhelming stack of value when subscribing to the Super App, while at the same time supporting an economic movement to restore Financial Justice by ending the Financial Matrix.

The Super App is built on the matchmaker business model, similar to companies like Uber and Airbnb, which provide a platform to introduce customers who want rides or rooms with people who have rides or rooms. These new *gig* economy matchmaker businesses are satisfying customers with lower prices and suppliers with increased sales and lower marketing costs, and they are themselves reaping the rewards for introducing the two groups. Although the matchmaker business model is not new (banks have been connecting people who have money with people who want money for thousands of years), through leveraging New Economy technologies (smartphones and apps), Uber, Airbnb, and their ilk have created multibillion-dollar businesses, blowing past rivals saddled with billions of dollars in hotel and automobile investments.

Likewise, Life's Super App is a New Economy matchmaker, allowing customers seeking to block the Financial Matrix to have fun, make money, and make a difference by connecting to suppliers who help them do so, all in one simple smartphone app. Furthermore, Life Members, representing the entrepreneurs we talked about in the geese example, are compensated for connecting customers to the platform. Everybody wins by tapping into the Super App—customers, members, and suppliers—everybody, that is, except the Financial Matrix. Moreover, a customer who operates a Main Street business can request to list their enterprise in the Super App's Coupon section, which gives them a double matchmaker benefit, by becoming both a customer and a supplier.

The Super App empowers the escape from the Financial Matrix by providing an alternative monetary platform where customers receive executive-level life benefits for being part of the Financial Justice movement. It offers immediate cash back, deep discounts on travel, credits toward dream vacations, discounts on shopping, coupons, education on finances and personal development, and so much more! The long-term objective is for the Super App to supply an alternative system to the oppressive Financial Matrix money and banking system (see Appendix II on "Free Market Money and Banking"), providing an escape route for freedom-loving people. Let's review each area of the Super App.

Have Fun

The Have Fun section of our Super App consists of deep discounts on travel, including airfare, hotels, and rental cars through our Thing or 2 Travel brand, and premier resort destinations worldwide through our Thing or 2 Resorts. Already competitive prices offered are then made more beneficial through something we call Trip Credits (TC). These have the value of 1 TC = $1 when applied toward hotel and resort stays. Monthly subscribers to the Super App, currently paying $30 US per month, are automatically awarded 30 TC each month, making their subscription to the app virtually free. Customers can also earn Trip Credits when purchasing products from the Super App's Marketplace. With no delays or minimums, customers can redeem these Trip Credits immediately toward outstanding travel deals or save and accumulate them for later.

Personally, I believe the vacation packages available through Thing or 2 Resorts are by themselves reason enough to subscribe to the Super App. I don't want to dive down too deep into the details, and, of course, these resort offers come and go based on availability, but the vacation deals are simply amazing. For instance, one that blew me away was a castle in Tuscany, Italy, which included bedrooms for six couples. It was located on a hillside overlooking spectacular views of the vineyards below, and the total price for seven nights in Tuscany, after redeeming several hundred Trip Credits (credits customers can earn in less than a year) was only $1,026! That's less than $25 per couple per night (less than your local Motel 6) for a dream vacation.

There are only around 12,000 registered timeshare resorts in the world, and approximately 10,000 of them are partnered with the Super App, but unlike the normal timeshare membership, wherein one pays thousands of dollars to join, every $30 Super App subscriber enjoys complete access without any hidden fees. Not surprisingly, many customers sign up just to save on their annual family vacation.

Make Money

The Make Money portion of the Super App consists of several ways that customers can save and earn money on normal, everyday purchases they were already going to make. The first is through our Coupon function, which includes over 350,000 in-store and over 230,000 mobile locations. These savings are immediate and are even *stackable* with other offers and discounts, including our own cash-back feature we'll discuss next. So step one for Super App customers, before making a purchase anywhere, is to check the Coupon section of the app to find out what deals are available.

As we like to remind customers, "Before going anywhere, check the app!" Step two is to check in the Groupon section of the app to see if that store is also offering any deals there. Third, customers then enter our Merchant section, in which nearly three hundred top national brands offer immediate cash back. A customer, either online or at the store, simply enters the amount of the purchase and selects a payment source (credit card, debit card, or cash previously placed into the Super App's convenient eWallet). The cash back, ranging from 1% to upward of 10%, is instantly placed in the customer's Super App for immediate future use.

If the payment source chosen is the money in the eWallet, then an additional 4% cash back is awarded in the form of Life's virtual currency called dibs. These are also instantly spendable at any of the roughly three hundred merchants inside the app. So as you can see, the savings and rewards in the Make Money section are stackable and can add up quickly! Further, by paying this way through the Super App, the whole process is touchless, an important consideration during a time of a global pandemic. And finally, the entire process is more secure, as the merchants never obtain your credit card information. As the reader can see, not only is the Have Fun section worth the $30 price, but so too is the Make Money section, and every month the value received goes up as more stores and coupons are added onto the Super App.

Make a Difference: Wealth and Personal Development Education

Finally, my personal favorite part of the Super App is the Make a Difference section. The Financial Matrix, as I have spent several chapters explaining, is hurting people and destroying dreams, so when Brady suggested we place our top-selling Financial Fitness Program (FFP) in the Super App at no extra cost, I was excited. The FFP is taught by individuals who have achieved a top 0.1% debt-free lifestyle. It consists of audios, videos, and e-books, all available digitally on the app and accessible at any time. Moreover, Brady also included Rascal Radio, the Pandora-like personal development library, featuring many *New York Times* best-selling authors, several internationally ranked leaders, and successful entrepreneurs in many diverse fields, contributing to over three thousand audio selections in all, again available at no extra charge. Previously, Life sold tens of millions of dollars of each of these products, but they are now provided as part of the incredible stack of value on the Super App. This ensures customers learn how to defend themselves against the Financial Matrix by applying financial literacy and leadership to everything they do. Many subscribers, after listening to this digital content, discover they love the Make a Difference section the best.

Make a Difference: Health Products

But that's not all for the Make a Difference category. Through the Super App Marketplace, we offer customers a chance to also take important steps toward improving and maintaining their health. As the saying goes, there is no true wealth without good health. Insofar as it is physically possible, cultivating a daily regimen including aerobic/anaerobic exercise, good nutrition, and proper rest is vital for a healthy immune system and longer life. Nevertheless, while nearly everyone acknowledges this, few practice it because busy lifestyles cause these things to be squeezed out. Harvard Health, for instance, said chronic inflammation was a major cause of the diseases plaguing humanity, including cancer, heart disease, diabetes, arthritis, depression, and Alzheimer's disease.[2] Furthermore, the list of foods contributing to this chronic inflammation includes refined carbohydrates (white bread and pastries), french fries (and other fried foods), soda (and other sugar-sweetened drinks), red meat (burgers, steaks) and processed meat (hot dogs, sausage), margarine, shortening, and lard.

The good news, according to Frank Hu, professor in the Department of Nutrition at Harvard, is that dietary habits have a huge impact: "Many experimental studies have shown that components of foods or beverages may have anti-inflammatory effects."[2] Such an anti-inflammatory diet includes tomatoes, olive oil, green leafy vegetables (such as spinach, kale, and collards), nuts like almonds and walnuts, fatty fish (like salmon, mackerel, tuna, and sardines), and fruits (such as strawberries, blueberries, cherries, and oranges).

The challenge, however, is that even though we know these things are good for us, we simply run out of time, money, and the focus required to consistently eat such good foods. Thankfully, there is a shortcut to improve our diet through nutritional supplementation. This closes the gap between our intentions and actions and ensures we receive the proper nutrients, vitamins, and antioxidants we need without spending hours a day to do so. Brady invested several years studying product claims and results, searching for those products that improved the immune system and overall quality of health. He and his team discovered a couple of companies doing it right—so right, in fact, that we partnered with them to make their products available through the Super App.

The first company, Zinzino, is based out of Norway, and offers a world-renowned Balance Oil product: a mixture of olive and fish oil that is scientifically designed to help balance the good omega-3s with the bad omega-6s in one's bloodstream. Zinzino is so confident in the efficacy of the Balanced Oil product that they encourage customers to take before-and-after blood tests to confirm for themselves their improvement in balanced health. Zinzino was an early pioneer discovering how to properly mix olive oil with fish oil to enhance the absorption rate of these essential nutrients in our bloodstream. This advancement has now been corroborated by an independent third party, PubMed, which concluded, "Ingestion of fish oil omega-3 fatty acids relieved several clinical parameters used in the present study. However, patients showed a more precocious and accentuated improvement when fish oil supplements were used in combination with olive oil."[3]

As an engineer, I love how PubMed's research scientifically verified what Zinzino learned experimentally (through thousands of blood tests), representing an impressive confirmation of theory with practice.

The second company, Mighty Muscadine, is located in North Carolina and is one of the top processors of the local muscadine grape, a fruit with an extra set of chromosomes to help it resist the heat and humidity of the Southern states where it grows. The muscadine grape has been a fan favorite in the South for years, with food recipes, local remedies, and legends of its healing powers passed on since the Indians occupied the land.

In the last decade, however, science is catching up with personal experiences. For example, a special edition of the *MD News* noted: "Muscadine grapes are fat free, high in fiber and they are high in antioxidants, especially ellagic acid and resveratrol. Ellagic acid has demonstrated anticarcinogenic properties in the colon, lungs and liver of mice. Resveratrol is reported to lower cholesterol levels and the risk of coronary heart disease."[4]

The muscadine grape is bursting with antioxidants, with impressive anti-inflammatory properties, most likely due to the extra set of chromosomes. And since Mighty Muscadine comes in capsules, busy customers can pursue better nutrition by simply taking the food supplement with meals. Interestingly, a North Carolina billionaire (not associated with the Mighty Muscadine company) anonymously donated $20 million to the Duke University Medical Center because he wanted to know the science behind the impressive results he had experienced personally. Muscadine grape extract and its effect on health across several categories have therefore been studied in vitro, in laboratory mice, and now in human clinical trials. As of the time of this writing, the study has entered its fifth year. There are fourteen peer-reviewed publications regarding muscadine grape extract and the research results found so far.

Further, the Super App partnered with CallonDoc, a web-based health-care platform created by licensed primary care physicians currently practicing medicine in the United States and soon in Canada. Any Super App customer enjoys 35% off normal prices, which can add up to big dollars, as simply another benefit of the Super App.

Super App Total Value

When we add up all the specific benefits within the Super App (and the previous discussion is by no means exhaustive of all that the Super App has to offer), one can see why the retention rate on the platform is high. After all, subscribers receive well over $100 in value for the $30 price. Let's run through the numbers. First, the $30 for the Super App is matched immediately with 30 Trip Credits, redeemable at 1 TC per $1 on the travel programs, making the Super App virtually free even if a person were to sign up and only use it on an annual vacation.

Moreover, depending on how often one goes shopping, the cash back per active user can range from $20 to $60, and for some even more, every month. When using the eWallet as the payment source instead of credit or debit cards, another $10 to $30 is added in, and this is before Coupons or Groupon. In fact, for Laurie and me personally, our $30 invested has consistently returned over $200 per month.

Naturally, we will continue subscribing to the Super App because with a return on investment of over 700% for being a customer, we would be foolish not to. Indeed, my recommendation is for customers to test out the Super App for themselves and calculate their return on investment. When customers discover it provides value multiple times the price, they will join the growing ranks of satisfied customers.

The Financial Fitness and Rascal Radio personal development programs are even greater because the return on investment of a debt-free life, with improved relationships and inner satisfaction from personal development, is incalculable. This is the most valuable aspect of the Super App. After all, wisdom is the great multiplier of results, and the thousands of testimonies from people who have gained financial wisdom to pay off credit cards, student loans, car loans, house mortgages, etc. is impressive, to say the least.

The value of the Super App is the key to the overall plan to help millions escape the Financial Matrix because satisfied customers want to share it with others. For some who begin sharing the Super App with others, it will make sense to take the next step and become an entrepreneur who gets paid to do so. This leads to the larger movement of freeing people from the Financial Matrix. Although everyone in North America should be on the Super App, even when just 10% of North American smartphone users become Super App customers, the result will be a multibillion-dollar movement, powered by a debt-free company intent upon setting people free from the Financial Matrix.

Becoming an entrepreneur should be hugely attractive to many people for several reasons. To survive in modern economies, one must earn money, and despite the thousands of potential careers, according to Robert Kiyosaki in *Cashflow Quadrant*, there are only four ways to earn money: as an employee, self-employed, business owner, or investor.[5]

Over the course of my life, I have earned income from each of these quadrants, and it's important to understand the upside rewards and downside risks of each one. First, identify which quadrant you are in currently, then which quadrant will help you live the life you've always wanted long-term, and then formulate a plan to help you get there. The biggest thing to understand about the four quadrants is that each represents a radically different way of earning money:

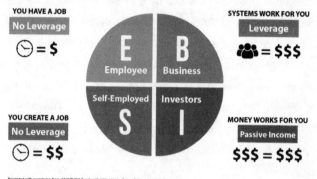

Employee Quadrant: "Per Hour" Pros and Cons

There is a common line of wisdom that says, "If you want to live your dreams, then you must work hard, get good grades, get a good job." While growing up in the small town of Columbiaville, Michigan, I must have heard this saying, without exaggeration, over a hundred times. I bought into its message and did all of the above, except the living the dream part! I quickly discovered that a good job provides security (at least in a good economy), since employees get paid regardless of the company's short-term profitability, but the price for security was paid by sacrificing opportunity. After all, employees sell time for money at a set price, which means doubling income in a year is, for all practical purposes, out of the question. Whereas entrepreneurs sacrifice short-term security for long-term opportunity, an employee does the opposite. Consequently, the employee quadrant is a great place to begin life, learning before earning, as I did as an engineer at AC SparkPlug, with a secure salary to wipe out my college debts and pay the bills, while developing entrepreneurial visions, beliefs, and habits.

Good employees cannot be paid what they are worth because, unlike entrepreneurs, they have taken little risk, therefore receive little upside reward. Thus, employees are a fixed cost for entrepreneurs, and normally the compensation is divided for most workers on a statistical bell curve. This leads to a situation in which good employees, in effect, subsidize bad employees. Salaries range between a few percentage points on a bell curve, even though Stephen Covey, the author of *The 7 Habits of Highly Effective People*, explained that workers practicing the proper habits can become thousands of times more effective than their peers.[6]

Of course, they will not see one thousand times the pay. Thus, the only people benefitting long-term from the employee quadrant are bad employees, who, whether they realize it or not, should appreciate being subsidized by their more productive peers. Lifetime employees are stuck on something we could call the *forty-five-year plan,* wherein, according to US Department of Labor data, income levels flatten out around age twenty-five and pay raises afterward merely cover the cost of living—until they retire, that is, when, despite now having free time, they are forced to try and get by on one-half to one-third of what they'd become used to while working.

For these reasons, I focused on growing myself, performing at top levels, and preparing to make my entrepreneurial leap. I realized staying in the employee quadrant would be selling myself short, and Laurie and I still had dreams that we knew we would not achieve if we stayed in our jobs.

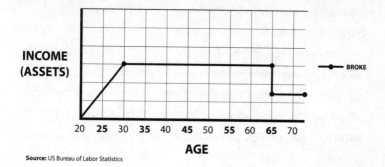

INCOME (ASSETS)

BROKE

AGE
20 **25** 30 **35** 40 **45** 50 **55** 60 **65** 70

Source: US Bureau of Labor Statistics

I still chuckle thinking about the first time I shared with my dad, a recently retired electrician, what I had learned about the forty-five-year plan. I was twenty-six years old and already doubting the employee quadrant when I told my dad I didn't think the forty-five year plan was working for me. He nodded his head and responded: "You know what, son? It didn't work for me either! I'm making half in retirement of what I made full-time." Ugh. Although I can laugh today, it wasn't funny at the time because it hit me like a ton of bricks that I had been taking advice from someone who didn't have the results I wanted. I loved my dad, and I knew my dad loved me, but a person is only qualified to give advice up to the level he has himself achieved. If I wanted to escape from the Financial Matrix, I needed to start taking advice from people who had escaped it. After eight years of schooling and working to become a successful engineer, I finally mentally shifted from being an engineer stuck in the forty-five-year plan to an entrepreneur on his way to leaving the Financial Matrix.

Self-Employed Quadrant: "Per Task" Pros and Cons

Self-employed people ought to be commended for having the courage to make the entrepreneurial leap, one that leads to potentially greater rewards in a free market. Most "S" business owners (doctors, homebuilders, lawyers, landscapers, accountants, etc.) get paid per service or task, which usually produces more money and control over their destiny, at least pre-COVID-19, than employees can obtain. In my case, after receiving a national technical benchmarking award, I left AC SparkPlug and moved into the "S" quadrant, making more money than ever before.

However, to grow that even further I would need to travel extensively, taxing my already limited schedule. At the time, with four young children, I was hesitant to do so. Furthermore, it didn't take me long to realize I had jumped out of the frying pan and into the fire. After all, since I was the one who developed the benchmarking process and won the award, the clients expected me to personally conduct the seminars. I soon discovered I had gone from one boss to many. In effect, I had traded a dollars-per-hour job for a higher-stress dollars-per-service business and was unfortunately still stuck trading time for money.

No wonder Kiyosaki said, "Never invest in a business where the system goes home at night,"[5] because I was the system going home exhausted! Although I was proud to own my own business, it soon became apparent that the business owned me. Indeed, as an "S" business owner, I felt like I was juggling bombs for money. The more bombs I juggled, the more money I made, but how many bombs could I juggle before one of them blew up? I knew there had to be a better way.

Business Owner Quadrant: "Per Relationship" Pros and Cons

Although the left-side quadrants can pay the bills and, as I said before, can be a great place to begin gaining income and experience, it is difficult to break out of the Financial Matrix because our time is finite. My breakthrough occurred when I finally understood the difference between my S-business and a B-business. The left side (per hour and per task) sells time to make money, which, by definition, is limited because there are only so many hours a person can sell in a day. The right side, in contrast, is not limited by time because the system produces the result, not the business owner.

This is why B-businesses are the key to escaping the Financial Matrix because, ultimately, they are the only endeavor that can scale beyond a 1:1 input of our time. Without multiplication, and even exponential leverage, an individual entrepreneur cannot grow big enough to have both the finances and time to unshackle himself or herself from the grips of the Matrix.

Perhaps an analogy will help highlight the key differences between left- and right-side strategies. Imagine a medieval town with a freshwater spring in the hills a half mile away and a person assigned to bring water into the town daily. An S-business would buy buckets, hire employees, and supervise the manual labor to ensure the team carried buckets to ensure the town had water. The need for water never ends, and in order to expand, the S-business would have to build another team and serve another village.

A B-business owner, on the other hand, would think systematically, and while carrying buckets to secure the contract in the short term, the long-term plan would be to create a water-delivery system, including a pump, a pipeline, and a gravity-fed system designed to deliver water continuously and without manual effort from the well to the town. Although this example is simplistic, the underlying point is not; any business owner who carries buckets to make money is trapped in an endless do-loop. To make more money, they must carry even more buckets.

The B-business owner builds and improves systems to produce the result without their daily involvement, freeing up their
mind to think of even more innovative systems to solve customer needs in the future. Whereas left-side thinkers focus on
carrying bigger and more buckets, right-side thinkers focus on
building bigger and more pipelines. The resultant lifestyle and
incomes, not surprisingly, are like night and day. Gerber wrote
about how Ray Kroc of McDonald's built a B-business system:

> Given the failure rate of most small businesses, he
> must have realized a crucial fact: for McDonald's to be
> a predictable success, the business would have to work,
> because the franchisee, left to his own devices, most
> assuredly wouldn't! Once he understood this, Ray Kroc's
> problem became his opportunity. Forced to create a
> business that worked in order to sell it, he also created
> a business that would work once it was sold, no matter
> who bought it. Armed with that realization, he set about
> the task of creating a foolproof, predictable business.
> A systems-dependent business, not a people-dependent
> business. A business that would work without him.[7]

Building a systems-dependent business was driven home
for me in November 1999, while listening to Michael Dell speak
at a Detroit Economic Club event. My epiphany occurred when
I realized how differently from me Dell viewed his business and
making money. Dell, after all, was only a couple of years older
than me, but there was a huge difference in financial results, with
his net worth over $20 billion and mine around $200,000. How, I
pondered, could Dell possibly be worth 100 million times more
than me? To be sure, I was willing to concede he was smarter and
perhaps worked harder (although I worked from dawn to dusk

back then), but even if he was ten times smarter and worked ten times as hard, that is still only one hundred times better, not 100 million times. Clearly, we were not on the same plane of thought when it came to businesses and money. The breakthrough occurred when I revisited *Cashflow Quadrant* and realized Dell was building a pipeline income, leveraging the system he created to build, market, and sell computers, whereas I was carrying big buckets and feeling exhausted. I realized, absurdly, that despite being a systems engineer who helped build manufacturing systems for clients, I did not apply systems thinking to wealth creation for myself. Archimedes, the famous Greek engineer, once said, "Give me a lever long enough, and a fulcrum to place it upon, and I will lift the world." It was time to build a lever long enough and a fulcrum to place it on for people to break free from the Financial Matrix.

When people use the Super App, they diminish the effects of Financial Matrix inflation by making and saving money, but to break free from it, they must develop a B-business. Life Members do this through sharing the Super App with others. Word-of-mouth marketing has proven again and again to be the best form of marketing any company can utilize. A recent McKinsey study identified word of mouth as the most effective form of marketing and advertising in the world, with word-of-mouth marketing generating double the sales revenue as paid advertising, and over 50% of all purchases were influenced by word of mouth.[8] But it has a catch: it only works if customers are truly enthusiastic about a product or service.

In the case of the Super App, we get to bypass expensive advertisements, endorsements, digital campaigns, and the like, because our Life Members get paid to do word-of-mouth marketing instead. They are compensated based on their performance, so no dollars are wasted in shot-in-the-dark scatter campaigns hoping to attract customers. We find that satisfied customers make the best Life Members because they have already become convinced of the value of the Super App, making it easy for them to share it with others. The simple three-step process of word-of-mouth marketing is:

1. Discovery: Somebody encounters a new idea.
2. Wow: This person is convinced that the idea is worth sharing.
3. Share: The person passes on the new information to others.

Naturally, once the process begins, the share stage for one person corresponds to the discovery stage for somebody else, and the word-of-mouth chain reaction has begun. Seth Godin, author of *Unleashing the Ideavirus*, underscored the importance of making it easy to share a company's product and message:

> How easy is it for an end user to spread this particular ideavirus? Can I click one button or mention some magic phrase, or do I have to go through hoops and risk embarrassment to tell someone about it? [9]

The Super App helps everyone Have Fun, Make Money, and Make a Difference and can be easily shared right from one's phone. It is simple, fun, systematic, and thus profitable. Every winning culture has a system to nurture it. Hungry students learn the fastest because they subscribe to Life's Marketing System (which teaches the specific techniques and principles of building a successful B-business sharing the Super App) and Standing Order Ticket (which provides monthly association with other successful and on-the-journey entrepreneurs through monthly seminars) to start their entrepreneurial adventure. The Super App platform paired with the Marketing System and Standing Order Ticket program supplies the best information Chris Brady and I have learned over the last twenty-five years on how to build a B-business.

Investor Quadrant: "Per ROI" Pros and Cons

The investor quadrant represents financially free multimillionaires who have escaped the Financial Matrix, having wiped out debts (including home mortgages) and built investments that produce cash flow and appreciate in value over time. This allows them to live indefinitely outside the trade-time-for-money-and-debt Financial Matrix trap. Every other quadrant invests time to make money (even the B quadrant must invest time and effort to develop pipeline thinking and skills), but the investor quadrant has transcended manual effort entirely, creating cash flow by money returning money.

Path To Financial Freedom

Get out of debt → Build pipeline income → Accumulate cash flow producing/appreciating assets

→

ESCAPING THE FINANCIAL MATRIX

Whereas compound interest works against most people, a situation in which they lose money while they sleep, those in the investor quadrant wake up wealthier because compound interest is working for them. As J. Paul Getty, the wealthy oil magnate, once emphasized, "The key to wealth is to learn how to make money while you sleep."[10] Those in the investor quadrant live debt-free, time-rich, and cash-flow lifestyles, freeing themselves from normal time constraints and allowing them the rare privilege of pursuing larger purposes and legacy-type goals. This should be the long-term aspiration of every reader (for more information, study our *Beyond Financial Fitness* program)—namely, to wipe out debts, build an ongoing pipeline income, and accumulate the cash-flow-producing assets to once and for all escape the Financial Matrix.

Cash . . . is to a business as oxygen is to an individual: never thought about when it is present, the only thing in mind when it is absent.

—Warren Buffett

Individuals don't win, Teams do.

—Sam Walton

CHAPTER 8

The Moonshot—The Three Keys to Wealth

We now have the road map to break free from the Financial Matrix. Knowing how debt enslaves people, we can break free by eliminating it and start the journey from trading time-for-money buckets to building pipeline systems of income. As mentioned, there are three business concepts essential to building a successful B-business and accumulating assets with cash flow. They are called the Three Keys to Wealth and are popularly remembered by the simple alliteration Literacy, Leadership, and Leverage. This is the path to escape and eventually help us eliminate the Financial Matrix:

1. Financial Literacy
2. Leadership Development
3. Leverage Systems

Nothing has the power to revolutionize a person's financial life as much as learning and living these concepts. When the Three Keys to Wealth become habitual, one can move from the bucket-carrying left side of the quadrant to the pipeline-income right side. Unfortunately, few realize the right-side quadrants exist, and for those who do, few of them have mentors to teach them the Three Keys to Wealth in order to take advantage of them. This is why I'm so excited about the Life Super App, because it provides the opportunity to learn how to build right-side quadrant wealth and be part of the Financial Justice movement in doing so.

Unlike a job, however, a B-business owner does not get paid until the business is systematically satisfying customers, and since systems can take years to perfect, lack of perseverance is the final frontier to succeeding on the right side of the quadrant. When applied to a sales process like marketing the Super App, the key to a great system is providing answers systematically rather than personally. This is because if people need to talk to the leader every time they have a question, there is nothing systematic about the process, and the leader's efforts are prohibited from scaling. Conversely, when an educational system teaching the best proven practices functions systematically, giving everyone the same information at the same time, then the leader's personal time can be more productively utilized in helping people expand their vision, replace limiting beliefs, and form the habits necessary to achieve their dreams.

Thankfully, Laurie and I realized that an opportunity to build a true B-business was very rare. This enabled us to settle in for the long haul, by understanding that something this valuable was going to take time and not be a *get rich quick* affair. We thus adopted a long-term view. After all, we reasoned, even if it took ten years (it actually took seven) to develop the vision, beliefs, and habits required to grow from the left side of the *Cashflow Quadrant* to the right side, the long-term gains would more than justify the short-term pains. One of my first mentors, a teacher in elementary school, used to say, "When the going gets tough, the tough get going."

I repeated that statement many times when the going got tough. Later, I developed a new saying: "You either hate losing enough to change, or you hate changing enough to lose." Indeed, I had plenty of fears when we first started, but I was even more fearful of losing because losing would sentence me to the Financial Matrix for life.

The Super App B-Business

The Super App is the entrepreneur's shortcut to B-business ownership. Every subscriber to the Super App is given access to our best-selling Financial Fitness (Financial Literacy) and Rascal Radio (Leadership Development) programs at no extra charge, providing the foundation to learn the first two keys to wealth. Between the audios, videos, and digital books for each program, subscribers learn the theory, knowledge, and practice to apply financial literacy and leadership development in their lives. Moreover, those who wish to fast-track learning the Three Keys to Wealth can also subscribe to the Life Accelerator, which provides access to every online webinar Brady and I have done or will ever do.

Life Accelerator is one of our most popular products because you pay once but enjoy the benefits for life. These webinars teach various aspects of the Three Keys to Wealth vital to move from the left-side to the right-side quadrants. The third key, Leveraging Systems, is taught in our Marketing System audios, videos, and live events. Members learn how to think entrepreneurially, sharing the Super App with others and leveraging the Life Marketing System to train hungry entrepreneurs in how to build pipeline incomes. Of course, the downside risk is minimal because this is a New Economy matchmaker business.

After all, the worst that happens to members is they are still satisfied customers, while the upside reward is an escape route from the Financial Matrix. The high customer retention rates, over 90% for those using the Super App, create secure and lucrative pipeline incomes, a dream B-business because it's a win for customers, a win for members, and a win for the companies participating on the Super App.

Entrepreneurs who leverage the Super App platform are applying all Three Keys to Wealth to build multiple streams of pipeline income through customers who Have Fun, Make Money, and Make a Difference. Leveraging systems is the key to explosive growth as Buckminster Fuller, one of the greatest systems thinkers of the twentieth century, explained in a 1972 interview:

> Something hit me very hard once, thinking about what one little man could do. Think of the Queen Mary—the whole ship goes by and then comes the rudder. And there's a tiny thing at the edge of the rudder called a trim tab. It's a miniature rudder. Just moving the little trim tab builds a low pressure that pulls the rudder around. Takes almost no effort at all. So I said that the little individual can be a trim tab. Society thinks it's going right by you, that it's left you altogether. But if you're doing dynamic things mentally, the fact is that you can just put your foot out like that and the whole big ship of state is going to go. So I said, call me Trim Tab.[1]

The trim tab is a great analogy for leveraging systems because it is a small rudder (in Fuller's example, on the rudder) that can turn 100,000-ton ships. Similarly, in a 1990 interview, a young Steve Jobs elaborated on the importance of leveraging systems for the advancement of the human race:

> I read a study that measured the efficiency of locomotion for various species on the planet. The condor used the least energy to move a kilometer. And, humans came in with a rather unimpressive showing, about a third of the way down the list. It was not too proud a showing for the crown of creation. So, that didn't look so good. But, then somebody at Scientific American had the insight to test the efficiency of locomotion for a man on a bicycle. And, a man on a bicycle, a human on a bicycle, blew the condor away, completely off the top of the charts. And that's what a computer is to me. What a computer is to me is it's the most remarkable tool that we've ever come up with, and it's the equivalent of a bicycle for our minds.[2]

Leveraging tools and systems, in other words, is the trim tab to advance societies economically. After all, there are only three ways to make money—namely, by addition, by multiplication, or exponentially—and the difference between the results of those three ways hinges on the amount of leverage applied. Addition could be compared to walking, multiplication to riding a bike, and exponential to anything from race cars to rockets.

The greater horsepower leveraged creates greater distances traveled per amount of human energy expended. For example, a significant majority of workers (around 90%) make money by addition. These people are in non-leadership positions with little educational or technical knowhow to differentiate themselves from the crowd. They are economic walkers in life, never getting very far because they have not learned to leverage skills.

In contrast, some people (close to 10%) make money by multiplication, having developed specific expertise and skills to differentiate themselves from the crowd, and thus are able to multiply their incomes accordingly. They are economic bikers in life, advancing much farther than the walkers because they have a little leverage.

However, the exponential crowd (about 0.1%) far surpasses the results of the other two groups because they have developed massive leverage economically through tools, technologies, and systems. Predictably, these people are winning the economic race because they are not walking or biking, but rather racing in high-powered cars or, if you like, even building rocket systems for their moonshot.

Whereas in addition $12 + 12 = 24$, and in multiplication $12 \times 12 = 144$, in exponential terms 12 to the 12th power $= 8.7$ trillion! Of course, developing the expertise and skills to reach exponential economic results takes time and effort, but the rewards are ridiculously better. It has always surprised me how few *zoom out* to realize the results are more than worth the investment. Entrepreneurs leveraging the Super App can achieve exponential results through community-wide learning. After all, as mentioned before, learning is one of the few things that compounds faster than interest.

Hungry learners become successful leaders through the daily application of something we refer to as Read, Listen, Associate, and Apply (RLAA). After all, we become like those we associate with, whether the association is through books, audios, videoconferences, or most impactfully, live events.

Speaker Charlie "Tremendous" Jones stated: "You will be the same person in five years as you are today except for the people you meet and the books you read."[3] The exponential mindset begins on the EDGE Call every Saturday morning. Just as Sam Walton ran his weekly Saturday-morning call to build his Walmart leadership team, the EDGE Call is a forum for LIFE entrepreneurs to celebrate achievements, learn the importance of goal setting, and develop the entrepreneurial mindset of exponential results.

Whereas specific techniques and approaches to building the Life business can be learned in a month or two, developing the entrepreneurial mindset to apply the Three Keys to Wealth routinely is a lifetime assignment. In other words, it's not the *how to* that holds people back as much as the *why to*. As Steve Jobs explained, vision is the ability to "zoom out," learning to begin with the end in mind:

> A lot of [what it means to be smart] is the ability to zoom out, like you're in a city and you could look at the whole thing from the 80th floor down at the city. And while other people are trying to figure out how to get from point A to point B reading these stupid little maps, you could just see it in front of you. You can see the whole thing. [2]

Visionary people, in other words, make connections that others cannot see, having the ability to *zoom out* to get a better perspective on the big picture. This is what the EDGE Call accomplishes for serious Life Members.

Vision not only ensures that one begins with the end in mind, it is also vital to entrepreneurial leadership. According to a 2015 study on creativity, openness to new ideas was revealed to be the best predictor for "job performance in situations requiring creativity." [4] The question becomes: What is the fastest way to increase the mind's openness to different experiences and ways of seeing the world? The answer is to become a lifelong reader.

Leaders from every field, including Harry S. Truman, Oprah Winfrey, and Elon Musk, among many, credit reading as the key to expanding their mental horizons. As a matter of fact, author Steve Siebold interviewed 1,200 of the wealthiest people in the world over the last thirty years and noted the common thread was how they bypassed TV and tabloids for personal development books. Siebold noted, "Walk into a wealthy person's home and one of the first things you'll see is an extensive library of books they've used to educate themselves on how to become more successful."[5]

Indeed, in my case, it was through a similar reading regimen, in which I devoured thousands of books, that led to the discovery and application of the Three Keys to Wealth we've been discussing. The two entrepreneurs who best modeled the Three Keys to Wealth and were instrumental in our wealth-building journey were Warren Buffett and Sam Walton. By beginning with the end in mind and *zooming out* to learn and apply key wealth principles habitually, these two men created massive ongoing results. Moreover, the wealth habits of these two, in particular, are what led to my understanding of the Three Keys to Wealth.

Warren Buffett: Financial Literacy — The First Key to Wealth

Warren Buffett is the best example of an I-quadrant investor and has compounded investments so successfully that he is one of the top five wealthiest people in the world. Although starting with little, he dreamed big, believed big, and disciplined his spending habits (minimized expenses) while carefully crafting his investment strategies (maximized investments) to compound assets. According to Warren Buffett, financial literacy is essential for success in the investor quadrant.

The simplest definition of financial literacy is the ability to live today on income earned yesterday so wealth can compound tomorrow. People who spend everything they make will never achieve wealth. Delayed gratification is the key to establishing enduring financial results, results that begin with saving as little as 5% of one's paycheck. Ironically, everyone practices delayed gratification of some type; the only question becomes: Is it internally motivated (having the money but not spending it) or externally motivated (not having the money and not spending)?

Everybody (outside of the Federal Reserve) has a limited amount of money and thus must practice delayed gratification, either internally or externally. The point is to quit spending today the money one hopes to make tomorrow because tomorrow's income is not as predictable as yesterday's. The destruction of our economy by the COVID-19 lockdowns has clearly demonstrated the precariousness of *tomorrow's income*.

After all, just as the possibility of drowning increases with every missed breath, so too does the possibility of bankruptcy with every missed payment. A person either practices internal delayed gratification and lives wealthier with time, or practices external gratification and lives poorer with time.

Another key strategy Buffett emphasized was to take financial advice only from those with proven results. Indeed, there are two surefire ways to financial failure: (1) listen to everyone, and (2) listen to no one. Laurie and I were stuck in the Financial Matrix because everyone we listened to was also stuck. How crazy is that? For if they truly knew how to escape the Financial Matrix, they probably would have taken their own advice before offering it to others.

Simply put, a person cannot mentor others in any area in which they have not achieved results themselves. If you haven't achieved the financial results you want, perhaps it's time to stop taking your own advice. One of my early mentors said that to me and it hurt, mainly because it was true of me. Wisdom is learned from knowledge, and knowledge is learned from experience, which is why learning from other people's experiences is the fastest way to wisdom.

Of course, this is why Laurie and I read, listened, and associated with successful people—to learn from their experiences. Since developing financial wisdom would take a lifetime of personal experiences, the shortcut is to learn it from other people's experiences. When it comes to money and finances, not surprisingly, I listen to Warren Buffett. For example, Warren Buffett once gave the following advice in a live CNBC interview in front of college students:

> CNBC: "What is the one thing that young people should be doing about money?"
>
> Buffett: "I tell them two things, generally. One is to stay away from credit cards. . . . The second thing I tell them is to invest in themselves." [6]

Buffett's short answer contains the two I-quadrant wealth keys: financial literacy and personal development, which is the beginning step of leadership development. Buffett emphasized knowing the difference between expenses and investments, which when not clearly understood, can lead to financial failure. Spending money when one should be saving or saving money when one should be investing are both significant wealth-reduction behaviors.

A friend of mine attended a luncheon with Warren Buffett where the financial sage recommended that young adults perform plastic surgery on their credit cards. He suggested sacrificing the plastic cards (with compounding interest over 15%) rather than sacrifice one's future wealth. Debt, according to Buffett, was financial cancer, a cancer he refused to invite into his finances, recommending, "If you're smart, you're going to make a lot of money without borrowing." If Buffett created wealth without debt, then so would the Woodwards, and so can you.

Warren Buffett: Personal Development — Part of the Second Key to Wealth

Leadership effectiveness is in evidence when a team's belief in tomorrow's vision is greater than today's reality. This creates the hunger to learn and grow the team's leadership, and leadership is the key upon which every organization rises and falls. The leader's belief in a better tomorrow, in effect, creates optimism in the future vision, propelling growth and change throughout the organization.

In contrast, when the leader's belief in tomorrow is low, it creates pessimism in the future vision and inhibits growth and change. Buffett was a strong proponent of personal and leadership development because he understood his investment was only as strong as the leaders within the companies. No wonder he encouraged saving as much as investing because minimizing self-consumption (expenses) made maximizing self-development (investments) easier.

In Buffett's two steps to building wealth, financial literacy is the necessary first step because it provides the funds for the second step, which is personal development. Buffett lives what he preaches. He once said he had no idea where his college degree was but proudly displayed his Dale Carnegie public speaking class certificate in his office, because he felt it was one of the best investments that he had ever made. Notice that this represents an investment in himself.

If the greatest investor in the world believed so strongly in the compounding effect of knowledge, I reasoned, then I should adopt lifetime learning as part of my belief system also. It's one of the best decisions I've ever made. Moreover, self-development is a daily habit, with Buffett once emphasizing the point by holding up a stack of reading materials and saying, "Read 500 pages like this every day. That's how knowledge builds up, like compound interest."[7]

Buffett also preaches constantly about the wonder of compound interest as it relates to money. After twenty-five years of compounding both learning and money, I have discovered there is only one thing more effective in creating wealth than compound interest, and that is compound learning. So to summarize, the fastest way out of the Financial Matrix is by compounding learning while also building a nest egg of money that compounds interest. It all begins with intentional personal growth. Personal development is a process, a habit someone should do for life, as Jim Rohn once noted: "Formal education will make you a living; self-education will make you a fortune."[8]

Sam Walton: Leadership Development— The Second Key to Wealth

Sam Walton took personal development to the next level by creating a learning organization through leadership development. Ironically, everyone sees how huge Walmart is today, but few remember its *David versus Goliath* origins. Indeed, in 1952 there were four new entrants into the discounting model. Three of them were backed by billion-dollar investors: Kmart (the Kresge fortune), Woolco (the Woolworth fortune), and Target (the Dayton-Hudson fortune); the fourth, Sam Walton, barely had enough money to open his first store, having to invest 95% of the money personally. Nonetheless, Sam Walton, the financial weakling in the battle with billionaires, won the battle hands down.[9]

How was this possible? The answer is leadership development, because Walton knew his business would grow when his leadership team did. As Peter Senge stated, "The only sustainable advantage is an organization's ability to learn faster than the competition."[10]

This is where Walton excelled: building leaders and results as good as any B-business owner of the twentieth century. He was relentless at developing leaders, because he knew he could not achieve his goals without them. Technology is important, but a technological advantage is not sustainable unless a company also creates a culture of learning throughout the organization. This is done through personal development and leadership growth and, when done correctly, becomes a sustainable advantage in itself. As Dale Carnegie noted in 1936: ". . . 15 percent of one's financial success is due to one's technical knowledge and about 85 percent is due to skill in human engineering—to personality and the ability to lead people."[10] Walton explained, "I needed somebody to run my new store, and I didn't have much money, so I did something I would do for the rest of my run in the retail business without any shame or embarrassment whatsoever: nose around other people's stores searching for good talent."[9]

And to Walton, talent meant hunger, for he knew only the hungry person would quickly learn from mistakes to grow as a leader. It is strange to me how few organizations focus on learning and leadership, especially when considering the ancient Chinese proverb that captured the principle thousands of years ago: "If you want one year of prosperity, grow grain. If you want ten years of prosperity, grow trees. If you want one hundred years of prosperity, grow people." Walton, in fact, went one better, for he didn't just grow people, he grew teams.

Understanding that talent without teamwork is disastrous, he went for both and encouraged leaders to "submerge your own ambitions and help whoever you can in the company. Work together as a team."[9] Walton modeled leadership, learning, and hunger everywhere he went, and the rest of the organization followed his lead. Once Walton had established a learning team, he next focused on vision and purpose, proclaiming, 'Communicate, communicate, communicate. . . . We do it in so many ways, from the Saturday morning meeting to the very simple phone call to our satellite system. The necessity for good communication in a big company like this is so vital it can't be overstated."[9] Finally, although Walton leveraged technology in gathering data and communicating messages, he never let *high tech* replace *high touch,* saying: "A computer is not—and will never be—a substitute for getting out in your stores and learning what's going on. In other words, a computer can tell you down to the dime what you've sold. But it can never tell you how much you could have sold."[9]

Those billion-dollar corporations that entered the space at the same time as Sam Walton did not stand a chance against his leadership team. After all, no matter how much they invested in high tech, Walton knew only high-touch leadership could inspire human beings to work together to achieve something bigger than themselves.

Sam Walton: Leveraging Systems —
The Third Key to Wealth

The first two keys to wealth, financial literacy and leadership development, make the third key to wealth, leveraging systems, possible. Financial literacy ensures the business has a healthy cash flow, while leadership development builds leaders. Then, the leaders create scalable systems, leveraged by teams of ordinary people, to consistently produce extraordinary results.

Whereas extraordinary efforts are not sustainable, building an extraordinary system in which ordinary efforts produce extraordinary results is. This is the second thing Walton did as well as any B-business owner: he followed the principle of leveraging systems to build a central scoreboard for his network of stores. This allowed him and others to centrally inspect the results he expected from his local-store leadership teams worldwide. Successful businesses eliminate chaos by creating reliable processes to produce predictable results.

Not surprisingly, in studying any billionaire's business model, one will discover a business system producing superior results consistently. The more predictable the business system, the more predictable the business results. Michael Gerber explained:

> Once the franchisee learns the system, he is given the key to his own business. Thus, the name: Turn-Key Operation. The franchisee is licensed the right to use the system, learns how to run it, and then "turns the key." The business does the rest. And the franchisees love it! Because if the franchisor has designed the business well, every problem has been thought through. All that's left for the franchisee to do is learn how to manage the system.[10]

Walton separated himself from the crowd by building a business system producing results even when he slept, which fellow retailer Abe Marks noted:

> He knew that he was already in what the trade calls an "absentee ownership" situation. That just means you're putting your stores out where you, as management, aren't. If he wanted to grow he had to learn to control it. So to service these stores you've got to have timely information: How much merchandise is in the store? What is it? What's selling and what's not? What is to be ordered, marked down, and replaced?

Walton was the visionary who realized how powerful re-al-time data was for absentee owners, who cannot be at every location at the same time. He described his philosophy:

> That's why I come in every Saturday morning usually around two or three [a.m.], and go through all the weekly numbers. I steal a march on everybody else for the Saturday morning meeting. I can go through those sheets and look at a store, and even though I haven't been there in a while, I can remind myself of something about it, the manager maybe, and then I can remember later that they are doing this much business this week and that their wage cost is such and such. I do this with each store every Saturday morning. It usually takes about three hours, but when I'm done I have as good a feel for what's going on in the company as anybody here—maybe better on some days.[9]

Walton led people and leveraged systems, building the most successful B-business of his age. Despite starting with little money compared to his billionaire competitors, Walton surpassed everyone by masterfully applying the Three Keys to Wealth, and his B-business has continued to thrive decades after he passed away.

Buffett and Walton changed our business mindset. No longer would we merely work hard to make money; instead, we would master the Three Keys to Wealth to achieve time and money freedom. The purpose was not to live pampered, unproductive lives, but rather to eliminate the urgent and replace it with a focus on the important. Indeed, one of the worst aspects of the Financial Matrix is that the urgent need for money overwhelms the important things in life. This is what building a B-business while flowing funds into the investor quadrant meant for us: time and money freedom to focus on making a difference by restoring Financial Justice to the world.

This is our moonshot opportunity, the chance to do something good that outlives all of us. However, to reach the moon, so to speak, nothing less than exponential results will do, for neither walking, biking, nor driving will get the job done. Instead, we must build a rocket ship for our moonshot. This is why we are so excited about the Super App platform. This is our chance to be part of something so big, so monumental, and so audacious that only a group committed to exponential rocket-ship results would even attempt it. Anything less than an exponential opportunity that reaches millions of people, needless to say, will not be capable of ending the Financial Matrix.

However, with the Super App, B-business owners can reach and teach millions of people how to apply the Three Keys to Wealth to escape the Financial Matrix personally but, more importantly, spread the Golden Rule Philosophy Free Market principles worldwide to end it globally. This is how we can restore Financial Justice to the people.

Fortunately, we now know how to build the platform for our moonshot. After all, the Three Keys to Wealth produce time and money freedom, and these are necessary for anyone aspiring to be a global influencer. In fact, as we will discuss in detail in the next chapter, the most important aspect is to believe it is possible, for as Dennis Waitley said, "If you believe you can, you probably can. If you believe you won't, you most assuredly won't."[13] Either way you are right. Over the years, I have observed that global influencers have five core characteristics in common that separate them from the crowd. World influencers have cultivated an approach to life that distinguishes them from the rest, who long to make a difference but never do so.

The first characteristic of world influencers is they believe in others, knowing every person can make a difference by defining his or her life around a compelling purpose. For me, Micah 6:8 became the defining purpose of my life: "He hath shewed thee, O man, what is good; and what doth the LORD require of thee, but to do justly, and to love mercy, and to walk humbly with thy God."

Call me crazy, but I dream of thousands of financially independent B-business owners who humbly seek justice and mercy, teaching millions of Super App customers how to have fun, make money, and make a difference in order to escape the Financial Matrix. Sure, B-business owners enjoy great lifestyles, but that is merely a side benefit.

What actually happens is that they come to realize that to whom much is given, much is required. Indeed, the Financial Matrix is nothing less than the greatest source of injustice in the world, and when community members set themselves free, they help others start their journey to freedom. To play any part in ending this injustice is noble, and to play a huge part in ending it is to become a world influencer.

This dream wakes me up in the morning, motivates me from dawn till dusk, and inspires me to teach others how to also break free. Perhaps you too were created for a time such as this and will play a huge part in ending the Financial Matrix.

The second characteristic of world influencers is they are lifetime learners (like Buffett and Walton were), constantly learning and growing to serve more people. The greatest leaders are voracious learners, reading, listening, and associating with greatness to improve in character, tasks, and relationships. Many people believe learning is boring, but one of life's big secrets is that learning can be just as enjoyable as entertainment, but with long-term benefits.

True learners are humble, realizing both that they can learn from anyone and that there is always more to learn. Furthermore, learning isn't about impressing others with how smart you are; rather, it's about impressing upon others how impactful their lives can be. This is why association with other learners is vital because, as Aristotle said, you are what you repeatedly do, and not surprisingly, you do what you repeatedly see being done. Children are born hungry learners, but standardized schooling drains that hunger, as Albert Einstein reputedly said, "We are born geniuses and taught to be idiots." Thankfully, a dream can relight the fire to learn, and learning can lead to a person transforming into a B-business world influencer, living the life they always wanted.

The third characteristic of world influencers is how they practice *imagination*: the ability to imagine and act simultaneously in order to create positive changes. Muhammad Ali once said, "The man who has no imagination has no wings,"[14] as if a person without imagination were like a bird with its wings clipped.

Sadly, too many are suffering from self-inflicted clipped wings because they are afraid to imagine a better future out of fear of failure. Without imagination, however, the fear of failure soon becomes a lifetime failure. Fortunately, past failures can be transformed into future successes the moment imagination is empowered, as Stephen R. Covey said, "Live out of your imagination, not your history."[15]

Nonetheless, imagination is not truly empowered until action is truly engaged because, as one of my college professors stated, "When all is said and done, much more is said, than ever done." Imaginaction is the coin, and imagination and action are the two sides. Tell me what a person is vividly imagining and acting upon, and I have the best predictor of their future. Walt Disney was a great dreamer, and he said, "All our dreams can come true, if we have the courage to pursue them."[16] To inspire others, a leader must live in imaginaction.

The fourth characteristic of world influencers is their ability to connect people of various races, creeds, and cultures together, uniting people around a common vision and purpose. Although many have vision to see with their eyes, only a few have vision to see with their minds. And, for every person with a compelling vision, a thousand will see it, and for every person who sees it, a thousand will act upon it. Therefore, one person with a compelling vision can launch the imaginaction process within millions of lives. After all, 1,000 X 1,000 is a million people.

A strong vision unites diverse people, and a united people can achieve practically anything because unity can make the weak strong, as the Ethiopian proverb states, "When spiders unite, they can tie down a lion." Force matrices, in other words, thrive by keeping the people divided, because they know the moment the people unite around economic liberty and justice, the Financial Matrix is over. The Golden Rule teaches us to respect one

THE MOONSHOT: THE THREE KEYS TO WEALTH 221

another's differences while magnifying one another's strengths, because that is how we would like to be treated. The dream to end the institutionalized injustice of the Financial Matrix should unite all people around Golden Rule principles. This is why the Bradys and Woodwards, instead of enjoying our comfortable B-business lifestyles, are dreaming and doing, building a rocket ship to take our moonshot opportunity to restore financial justice to a financially oppressed world.

The fifth, and final, characteristic of world influencers is they focus on leaving the world a better place than they found it. The principle is "When you have been blessed, become a blessing." In a free market, the more you serve, the more you deserve, because honorable wealth is created through service to others. Furthermore, because leaders exponentially increase results through leverage, they must remember to whom much is given, much is required.

After all, as wealth increases, so does the power to do good and evil. Thus, instead of the people relying on angelic leaders to always do right, perhaps it would be wiser for society to insist on limited funds to ensure funds are not available to create an absolute power. To leave the world a better place than we found it, in this instance, world influencers must focus on ending institutionalized absolute power. After all, it takes money to enforce power, which is why limited funds have always led to limited power and unlimited funds have always led to unlimited power.

The Financial Matrix was given unlimited funding through the creation of fiat money, and the potential for absolute power has now become a reality. It's time to limit central banks' ability to create unlimited amounts of fiat money in order to end the Financial Matrix's absolute power. This will set the people and states free.

Anyone can be a world influencer, but it takes faith to get started, persistence to stay the course, and constant growth to overcome obstacles, no matter what. Like my friend Dan Hawkins learned, when you get up to bat you must take a swing to make something happen.[17]

For instance, in Bedford, England, a statue stands of a poorly educated tinkerer, a metalworker, who joined the army at age sixteen but became the author of the most widely read English book (except the Bible) for over three centuries. Indeed, until the twentieth century, it was one of the first books purchased in English-speaking homes and a common sight on bookshelves along with the Bible. The statue is of John Bunyan, a man who spent twelve years of his life imprisoned, punished because he dared to preach the Gospel message without having the proper state certification. The Lord Judge Magistrate of Bedford, convinced that this would shut the mouth of this common tinkerer, said at his sentencing: "At last we are done with this tinker and his cause. Never more will he plague us: for his name, locked away as surely as he, shall be forgotten, as surely as he. Done are we, and all eternity with him."[18]

No statement could have been further from the truth, because this uneducated tinkerer did not stay quiet. Bunyan decided that if imprisonment forbade him from speaking Gospel truths, then he would write them instead. In 1675, Bunyan wrote *The Pilgrim's Progress*, now translated into over two hundred languages. Samuel Johnson commented on the popularity of Bunyan's book: "This is the great merit of the book, that the most cultivated man cannot find anything to praise more highly, and the child knows nothing more amusing."[19]

Ironically, Bunyan was offered freedom from prison provided he refrain from preaching. But he famously replied, "If you release me today, I will preach tomorrow." And so he remained in his dank cell and wrote the best-selling allegorical novel of all time. No magistrate, no prison, nor any punishment could silence the purpose John Bunyan had in his heart to share the Gospel message with others. Likewise, people realizing the injustices of the Financial Matrix can decide to take principled stands and become world influencers right from their own positions in life. One doesn't need to be locked up in order to make a difference; one merely needs to stand up.

As long as our government is administered for the good of the people, and is regulated by their will; as long as it secures to us the rights of person and of property, liberty of conscience, and of the press, it will be worth defending.

—President Andrew Jackson

CHAPTER 9

Breaking the Financial Matrix Paradigm

A paradigm is a standard, perspective, or set of ideas—a specific way of looking at something. Paradigms help us make sense of the world, playing an essential part in our worldview, how we see the world. In consequence, paradigm shifts are revolutionary to persons and societies because they change our perspectives on what we are experiencing in life. For example, in the mid-nineteenth century, Ignaz Philipp Semmelweis launched an antiseptic paradigm shift in the medical field while working in the maternity wards of the Vienna General Hospital. His research eventually led to the replacement of the now-obsolete miasma theory (pollution in the air causes diseases) with the germ theory (microorganisms known as pathogens or "germs" can lead to disease).[1]

Semmelweis supervised the two maternity clinics in the hospital, one served by medical students, the other by midwives. Because he had specialized in statistical methods at the University of Vienna, Semmelweis began recording the results achieved in both clinics. He was shocked to discover the death rate of mothers in the first obstetrical clinic was 13.10%, significantly higher than the 2.03% of the second one. Tellingly, the miasma theory could not account for such a radical difference in the data, since the air quality at both clinics was identical. Semmelweis, as a result, closely studied puerperal fever (commonly known as "childbed fever"), the leading cause of the high maternal and neonatal mortalities, looking for clues to the wide discrepancy in death rates. His breakthrough occurred, tragically, while attempting to save his doctor friend, who had been accidentally poked by another student's scalpel during an autopsy. Semmelweis stayed at his friend's bedside and noticed his symptoms were similar to the childbed-fever mothers. This insight helped him realize that medical students who were performing dissections on dead bodies and then going upstairs to help women deliver babies were somehow taking contamination with them.

Although this is common sense today, it was a revolutionary conclusion to draw back then. The students performing both dissection and baby-delivery tasks weren't washing their hands between procedures! Semmelweis's discovery scientifically explained why the second clinic's death rate was so much lower than the first. After all, the midwives were not operating on cadavers like the medical students. Semmelweis confirmed that puerperal sepsis, the childbed fever suffered by mothers, could be prevented if doctors simply washed their hands with chlorinated lime solutions. Implementation of his methods immediately reduced the number of cases of fatal puerperal fever from 12.24% to 2.38%, and many months there were no deaths from childbed fever at all. This was the beginning of the antiseptic era.

Semmelweis, in short, had proposed a new paradigm, the germ theory, to account for the radical differences in death rates. However, his theory was not accepted until decades later because the miasma paradigm was too solidly entrenched. The medical establishment simply refused to accept the self-evident data presented to them. Rather than admit they were inadvertently responsible for their patient's deaths, they challenged the research and researcher instead. In fact, Semmelweis's superiors were so upset at his breach of etiquette, he was unceremoniously tossed from the Vienna General Hospital in 1849, fired for daring to suggest the current medical paradigm was not only erroneous, but deadly. Unprepared for the level of backlash and criticisms he suffered for the next fifteen years, Semmelweis's health broke down. By 1865, he was committed to an asylum, suffering from depression, and died. Alas, what is common sense today was once an unforgivable heresy that drove its discoverer to an early grave. Fortunately, the truth always wins out in the end, and his antiseptic methods led to the germ theory being the accepted medical paradigm.

Even in scientific pursuits, where the endless quest for knowledge demands open-mindedness, data that causes the ruling paradigm to be questioned is vehemently resisted. Philosopher of science Thomas Kuhn described how normal science "is predicated on the assumption that the scientific community knows what the world is like," and that "scientists take great pains to defend that assumption." As a result, Kuhn observed science "often suppresses fundamental novelties because they are necessarily subversive of its basic commitments." Nonetheless, paradigm shifts cause scientific revolutions when the unexplainable anomalies, as Kuhn explains, "subvert the existing scientific tradition," and the old paradigm collapses.[2] The greatest scientific advancements, as is true in every field, are the result of paradigm shifts. The Copernican Revolution, for instance, advanced our understanding of the solar system. This was a paradigm shift from the now-obsolete Ptolemaic model of the heavens, which described the cosmos as having Earth stationary at the center of the universe, to the heliocentric model with the sun at the center of the solar system.

Not surprisingly, the Copernican Revolution was greatly resisted, like every paradigm shift, by those who were educated, recognized, and rewarded in the old paradigm. Shifts in thinking are not for the timid, as Arthur Schopenhauer communicated when he observed: "All truth passes through three stages. First, it is ridiculed. Second, it is violently opposed. Third, it is accepted as being self-evident."[3] Before judging medical and scientific experts too harshly, it's important to realize that paradigm shifts are extremely uncomfortable for all of us. Shooting messengers is much easier than thinking through new data. Despite many of the greatest advancements in humanity occurring during paradigm shifts, the truth is, as Friedrich von Hayek noted, "Nothing is more securely lodged than the ignorance of the experts."[4]

Few people enjoy admitting when they are mistaken, especially when considered experts. All of us tend to react like Semmelweiss's superiors, resisting the truth that would set us free. To the point, the Financial Matrix is a woefully inadequate and inaccurate financial paradigm. However, since the Financial Matrix Media runs the educational system, we have been immersed within its paradigm. And similar to Semmelweiss, those who propose a more truthful paradigm will meet resistance from the entrenched experts.

Nonetheless, when total debts are four times higher than the total money supply worldwide, and the gap continues to expand indefinitely, it is only a matter of time before the current financial system is exposed as fraudulent. Free people are not meant to be perpetual debt peons of the financial elites. It's time for a financial paradigm shift to restore liberty, justice, and prosperity. As we discussed in an earlier chapter, there are only two economic paradigms: either the Power Rule Philosophy (PRP) force matrix or the Golden Rule Philosophy (GRP) free market.

Since 1971, the Financial Matrix has parasitically yoked itself to the global economy and inflated the money supply at will.

The debilitating results have led to an explosion in money supply, total debts, and business boom/bust cycles in 2008 and 2020 that threatened to collapse the banking system and world economy. The explanation for the continued political support of such a volatile money system is found in the Financial Matrix's ever-increasing grip over Money, Media, Management, and Monopolies, which ensures that few are aware of any alternative. Nonetheless, the monetary fallacies and failures inherent within the Financial Matrix are steadily being exposed as the economic data is revealing the bankruptcy of the force matrix financial paradigm.

However, if Semmelweiss's medical paradigm shift was greatly resisted when only pride was on the line, how much more will a new financial paradigm be resisted when expert pride is combined with excess profits? The Financial Justice movement has exposed not only the systemic fallacies of fractional reserve banking, but also how it has institutionalized injustice. The Financial Matrix will not support Financial Justice any more than a poker player holding four aces will support a redeal. And the Federal Reserve is not apologetic about its position, as former chair Alan Greenspan boasted, "There is no other agency of government which can overrule actions that we take."[5]

The current chair, Jerome Powell, took this to heart. Speaking before the US House Committee on Financial Services, he acknowledged the monetary innovations and benefits of cryptocurrencies and digital dollars, but then added, "This is something that the central banks have to design. . . . The private sector is not involved in creating the money supply, that's something the central bank does."[6] Nothing more clearly demonstrates the opposing economic paradigms (force matrices versus free markets) than the above statements.

The Financial Matrix is as ubiquitous as it is iniquitous because it is the only monetary game worldwide. And the way it maintains absolute power is by overt violations of free market principles in the money and banking areas. And, while working for money is honorable, being forced into debt servitude in a cruel game of musical chairs is unworthy of a civilized nation. Every worker deserves Financial Justice, but to achieve this we must end the Financial Matrix's absolute power. This is why we need a paradigm shift, for without freedom in the money and banking sphere, we are unjustly hindered from building a fully functional alternative economic platform that can compete against the Financial Matrix and win.

After all, reasoning with the Financial Matrix is like playing chess with pigeons. No matter how carefully one explains the rules of the game, the systematic movement of the pieces, and the strategic objectives, the pigeons merely crap on the board, knock down the pieces, and strut around claiming they've won. The financial pigeons have made a mockery of limited government, free markets, and fiscal sanity because money is no longer subjected to market forces and economic law, but instead to political forces and economic greed. The Financial Matrix is the worldwide injustice of our age, which supports nearly every other injustice.

"Ideas have consequences,"[7] as Richard Weaver observed, and wrong ideas always lead to wrong consequences. The wrong consequences, in this case, are the worldwide Financial Matrix injustices. The fractional reserve banking system creates instability in the money supply, and no matter how many interventions are tried, the elites cannot stabilize the inherently unstable system. Murray Rothbard, among many, noted:

Before the Industrial Revolution in approximately the late 18th century, there were no regularly recurring booms and depressions. There would be a sudden economic crisis whenever some king made war or confiscated the property of his subjects; but there was no sign of the peculiarly modern phenomena of general and fairly regular swings in business fortunes, of expansions and contractions.[8]

This is not a coincidence since fractional reserve banking became the standard banking operation during the birth of the Industrial Revolution and after the period referred to by Rothbard. The seed of today's economic destruction was planted with the complete adoption of the FRB system, and until this seed is removed, the world's economies will continue to unfairly exploit the people. Thankfully, as people realize the Financial Matrix is the root cause of their loss of liberty, justice, and prosperity and that there is a free market alternative, the Financial Matrix will end.

In reality, as discussed in my *And Justice For All* series, the story of Western civilization is the quest for concord: the proper balance between the opposing philosophies of force and freedom within society. Like a pendulum at rest, concord is achieved when society enjoys freedom with force applied only to ensure justice for all under law. Not surprisingly, concord is extremely difficult to achieve and even more difficult to maintain.

When too much force is applied, the pendulum swings society into coercive tyranny, but when too little force is present, the pendulum swings society into chaotic disorder. This struggle is not new. Ancient historian Herodotus, writing about the Greco-Persian wars, realized way back then that what was really going on in those wars was a battle between opposing force and freedom philosophies. Western civilization's history is a continuation of this theme, with each subsequent generation striving to achieve concord between force and freedom doctrines. Accordingly, America's founders worked strenuously to attempt to balance these two opposing philosophies when constructing their new nation.

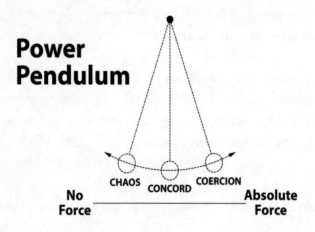

Power Pendulum

CHAOS CONCORD COERCION

No Force _____ **Absolute Force**

On one side, Alexander Hamilton promoted the Power Rule Philosophy, and on the other, Thomas Jefferson promoted the Golden Rule Philosophy. These two men and their competing philosophies battled for America's soul, and the outcome would determine if America would be an Empire of Freedom or an Empire of Force. Jefferson envisioned America as an Empire of Freedom, wherein people would enjoy liberty and justice for all under a limited government. President Jefferson summarized his political philosophy in his first inaugural address:

> [A] wise and frugal government, which shall restrain men from injuring one another, shall leave them otherwise free to regulate their own pursuits of industry and improvement, and shall not take from the mouth of

labor the bread it has earned. This is the sum of good government.[9]

It followed that the GRP Free Market was strongly defended throughout the nineteenth century under the presidencies of Madison, Jackson, and Van Buren, who agreed with Jefferson. Hamilton, in contrast, envisioned America as an Empire of Force (specifically financial force through a central bank similar to the Bank of England's role in the British Empire), wherein the elites siphoned the wealth of the people. As author Thomas Dilorenzo emphasized, Hamilton "was a frenetic tax increaser and advocated government planning of the economy. He championed the accumulation of public debt, protectionist tariffs, and politically controlled banks; belittled politicians like Jefferson who spoke too much of liberty; and believed the new American government should pursue the course of national and imperial glory, just like the British, French, and Spanish empires." [10]

The PRP force matrix was strongly promoted by Henry Clay, who picked up Hamilton's mantle, and again later by Abraham Lincoln. The problem with the state (public sector funds) supporting the force matrix, as Austrian economist Murray Rothbard so aptly described, is:

Far from adding cozily to the private sector, the public sector can only feed off the private sector; it necessarily lives parasitically upon the private economy. But this means that the productive resources of society—far from satisfying the wants of consumers— are now directed, by compulsion, away from these wants and needs. The consumers are deliberately thwarted, and the resources of the economy diverted from them to those activities desired by the parasitic bureaucracy and politicians. In many cases, the private consumers obtain nothing at all, except perhaps propaganda beamed to them at their own expense.[11]

President Andrew Jackson followed in Jefferson's footsteps and Senator Henry Clay followed Hamilton's. The highwater mark for the Golden Rule Philosophy and freedom and prosperity in America (regrettably, not for all people groups) was Jackson's victory over Henry Clay in the battle of the Second Bank of the United States. Less than two hundred years ago, Jackson ended central banking in America and significantly limited fractional reserve banking as well.

Jackson was a *hard money* (precious metal money) man from the beginning of his political career, having lost extensive landholdings after the Panic of 1796–1797 due to massive FRB inflation and deflation of banknotes. Jackson was elected president on a platform that was strongly opposed to central banks, national debts, and the FRB *unconstitutional banking,* as he described it to his friend William B. Lewis. Arthur Schlesinger Jr. records a public speech given by Amos Kendall, one of President Jackson's most trusted advisers, which effectively declared war on the financial force matrix in support of free markets:

"In all civilized as well as barbarous countries," he declared, "a few rich and intelligent men have built up Nobility Systems; by which under some name, and by some contrivance, the few are enabled to live upon the labor of the many." These ruling classes, he said, have had many names—kings, lords, priests, fundholders, but all "are founded on deception, and maintained by power. The people are persuaded to permit their introduction, under the plea of public good and public necessity. As soon as they are firmly established, they turn upon the people, tax and control them by their influence of monopolies, the declamation of priestcraft and government-craft, and in the last resort, by military force." Was America immune from this universal pattern? "The United States," said Kendall ominously, "have their young Nobility System. Its head is the Bank of the United States; its right arm, a protecting Tariff and Manufacturing Monopolies; its left, growing State debts and States incorporations.[12]

Kendall, in 1832, had already spelled out the structure of today's Money, Media, Management, and Monopoly Financial Matrix. Nonetheless, Kendall's and Jackson's views didn't alarm Nicholas Biddle, the president of the Second Bank of the United States (the central bank of America) because politicians rarely keep campaign promises once elected. Biddle, a scion of Philadelphia high society, believed in the Power Rule Philosophy force matrices and loathed common people. Jackson, in contrast, was a self-made frontier man who believed in Golden Rule Philosophy free markets and was the people's favorite. Biddle and Jackson held competing visions for America, one believing in predestined wealth, the other in equal opportunity.

The first salvo of what came to be known as the Bank War was President Jackson's first presidential message, in which he said: "Both the constitutionality and the expediency of the law creating this bank are well questioned by a large portion of our fellow citizens, and it must be admitted by all that it has failed in the great end of establishing an uniform and sound currency." Biddle, however, still believed Jackson was posturing and responded to the attack with a cool indifference: "They should be treated as the honest though erroneous notions of one who

intends well." [12] Nonetheless, as a precaution Biddle strength-
ened the Bank's political support, offering numerous perks and
privileges to anyone in Congress willing to aid the Bank's rechar-
ter, even successfully recruiting Henry Clay and Daniel Webster,
both senatorial demigods, to assure smooth sailing in the upcoming Bank renewal process.

The senators suggested renewing the charter early, smugly
concluding the president would capitulate when he saw the size
and power of the conglomerate arrayed against him, especially
with his reelection at stake. Capitulation, as the British had discovered in the Battle of New Orleans, was not part of Jackson's
nature, and surrendering to what he perceived to be injustice
was even more alien to his character.

The Bank advocates underestimated Jackson, and, despite
the senators navigating the Bank bill through Congress, Jackson
vetoed it and effectively declared war on the financial elites. The
historic veto message includes:

> It is to be regretted that the rich and powerful
> too often bend the acts of government to their selfish
> purposes. Distinctions in society will always exist
> under every just government. Equality of talents, of
> education, or of wealth can not be produced by human
> institutions. In the full enjoyment of the gifts of Heaven
> and the fruits of superior industry, economy, and virtue,
> every man is equally entitled to protection by law; but
> when the laws undertake to add to these natural and
> just advantages artificial distinctions, to grant titles,
> gratuities, and exclusive privileges, to make the rich richer
> and the potent more powerful, the humble members of
> society—the farmers, mechanics, and laborers—who
> have neither the time nor the means of securing like

favors to themselves, have a right to complain of the injustice of their Government. There are no necessary evils in government. Its evils exist only in its abuses. If it would confine itself to equal protection, and as Heaven does its rains, shower its favors alike on the high and the low, the rich and the poor, it would be an unqualified blessing.

Jackson was not only courageous, but also knowledgeable. He had studied stock manipulations, boom/bust cycles, and fractional reserve banking extensively. Because he understood inflation was fraudulent, Jackson refused to be hornswoggled by the bank's power brokers. Realizing the danger, Biddle now pulled out every political maneuver in the book to defeat the president's intransigence.

He purchased space in newspapers across America for a series of propaganda pieces refuting, or at least obfuscating, Jackson's veto message, encouraging one editor, "If you will cause the articles I have indicated and others which I may prepare to be inserted in the newspaper in question, I will at once pay to you one thousand dollars." [13] A thousand dollars at the time was worth around forty thousand dollars today, certainly enough to encourage many editors to comply.

More surprisingly, however, was Daniel Webster's support of the Bank. One of the nation's best legal minds, Webster had strongly opposed the Bank on constitutional grounds when it was originally proposed. Now, he was avidly supporting the renewal of the Bank in the Senate. Perhaps the reason Webster changed positions is revealed in a letter he sent to Biddle: "I believe my retainer has not been renewed or refreshed as usual. If it be wished that my relation to the Bank should be continued, it may be best to send me the usual retainers." [13] Evidently,

Biddle's payment of Webster's healthy retainer fees helped him overcome any constitutional scruples, and in this light, his criticisms of Jackson are not surprising.

Biddle left no stone unturned, issuing loans, retainers, and outright gifts to members of Congress to buy influence and overwhelm Jackson with sheer numbers. This was a battle for the nation's financial soul, and the stakes were extremely high, with the presidential election and billions in bank profits on the line. The battle turned in Jackson's favor, however, when he withdrew the Treasury deposits (the government's tax revenues) from the Bank, effectively starving it.

Biddle was aghast when he heard the news, exclaiming to Webster, "They will not dare to remove them. If the deposits are withdrawn, it will be a declaration of war which cannot be recalled."[13] Biddle was now desperate, having only one more ace up his sleeve, an economic assault upon America. In complete disregard of the millions of innocent people who would be economically crushed by Biddle's manipulations, he began strategically foreclosing on loans to cause a nationwide panic.

Despite the loans not being in arrears, Biddle demanded the Bank's money back in full,[13] which collapsed the money supply and bankrupted families, businesses, and local banks and governments. The clamor from the victims of Biddle's coldhearted callousness, who essentially begged the president to give in, nearly turned the tide in Bank's favor. Biddle was certain Jackson would restore the Treasury deposits to relieve the pressure on his constituency and wrote:

> My own view of the matter is simply this. . . . The [instigators] of this last assault on the Bank regret and are alarmed by it. But the ties of party allegiance can only be broken by the actual conviction of existing

distress in the community. Nothing but the evidence of suffering abroad [that is, in the country as a whole] will produce any effect in Congress. . . . This worthy President thinks that because he has scalped Indians and imprisoned judges, he is to have his way with the Bank. He is mistaken.[13]

Biddle, however, was the one who was mistaken.[14] To Jackson, this only confirmed that the unelected and unconstitutional power of the central bank over America must end, no matter the price, for any power capable of causing nationwide panics in which the common man suffers from the selfish moves of the elites is antithetical to liberty and justice. Jackson explained:

The Bank has by degrees obtained almost entire dominion over the circulating medium, and with it, power to increase or diminish the price of property and to levy taxes on the people in the shape of premiums and interest to an amount only limited by the quantity of paper currency it is enabled to issue.[14]

Biddle now lost his poise, openly admitting how money is used to influence politics, writing, "In half an hour I can remove all the constitutional scruples in the District of Columbia: Half a dozen presidencies (of bank branches), a dozen cashierships, fifty clerkships, a hundred directorships, to worthy friends who have no character and no money."[13]

Despite such a willingness to drop to any level in order to win, Biddle lost the Bank War, mainly because he had never squared off against a politician who could not be bought at any price. He kept believing Jackson would buckle, writing to another confidante, "My own course is decided, all other banks and all other merchants may break, but the Bank of the United States shall not break."[13] Biddle discovered that Jackson followed his principles, not profits, no matter how powerful the opposition. Jackson told his vice president, Martin Van Buren, "The Bank is trying to kill me. But I will kill it."[15] True to his word, President Andrew Jackson, near the end of his second term, was able to boast, like no other president before or since has been able to do: "We have no emergencies that make banks necessary to aid the wants of the treasury; we have no load of national debt to provide for, and we have on actual deposit a large surplus."[16]

Jackson knew people cannot live free under a centralized and controlled money and banking system, and neither can we. Unfortunately, however, by the twentieth century, like a phoenix rising from the ashes, the PRP financial force matrix once again achieved ascendancy.

In 1913, America adopted a force matrix banking and money system with the advent of the Federal Reserve. And as with all force matrix paradigms, the elites were thereby legally permitted to plunder the people's liberty, justice, and property, by siphoning from production to gain profit and power. Between World War I (1914), the Great Depression (1929), World War II (1939), and the 1971 end of the gold standard worldwide, the twentieth century was a banner time for the Financial Matrix elites.

Despite every historical example of absolute power force matrices ending badly, since 1971 the Financial Matrix, like a supernova, has drawn all other powers into its orbit. And even though the supernova may burn brightly temporarily, it does so by consuming people's wealth. The Financial Matrix will not burn out until it bankrupts the people. Such a perverse arrangement is intolerable.

In fact, if the financial truths shared in this book were widely known, it wouldn't be tolerated. Russian historians Mikhail Heller and Aleksandr Nekrich described how the Soviet Union enslaved its people, and these same methods apply equally to the Financial Matrix on a global scale:

> From time immemorial history has been written by the victors. "Woe to the vanquished," said the ancient Romans, by which they implied not only that the vanquished may be exterminated or turned into slaves but that the conquerors write the history of their wars; the victors take possession of the past and establish their control over the collective memory.[17]

George Orwell, perhaps the only Western writer who profoundly understood the essence of the Soviet world, devised this precise and pitiless formula: "Whoever controls the past controls the future."[18]

Orwell was not the first to say this, though. Mikhail Pokrovsky, the first Soviet Marxist historian, anticipated Orwell when he wrote that history is politics applied to the past. The Financial Matrix is the victor, and to the victor belong the spoils. Heller and Nekrich also noted how the Soviet Union's Communist elites used the state to propagandize, explaining education "was placed at the service of the state to the greatest possible extent and in the most conscious, systematic way. After the October [Communist] revolution not only the means of production were nationalized but all spheres of existence, and above all, memory, history. Memory makes us human. Without it people are turned into a formless mass that can be shaped into anything the controllers of the past desire."[17] The Soviet state systematically rewrote the Russian people's past in order to control its future. Soviet historian Maxim Gorky boasted, "We must know everything about the past, not in the way it has been written about heretofore; but rather, in the way it appears in the light of the doctrine of Marx-Engels-Lenin-Stalin."[17]

Just as the Soviet Union supernova (1917–1991) rewrote history to maintain its absolute power over the Russian people, so too does the Financial Matrix rewrite world history. The Financial Matrix is a global absolute power and cannot risk people awakening to the truth. Professor Robert Hutchins warned of this danger in his *Great Books* series preface:

> The reiteration of slogans, the distortion of news, the great storm of propaganda that beats upon the citizen twenty-four hours a day all his life long mean either that democracy must fall prey to the loudest and most consistent propagandists or that the people must save themselves by strengthening their minds so that they can appraise the issues for themselves.[19]

There are only two paths to choose from here: either we restore Financial Justice by ending the force matrix, or we continue to be exploited mercilessly out of the hard-earned fruits of our labor. In *The Politics of Obedience*, Étienne de La Boétie explained how it is in the nature of people to desire freedom and responsibility, yet they are instinctively molded by their cultural surroundings.

The Financial Matrix has molded people into believing financial serfdom is normal, and as Boétie stated, they "grow accustomed to the idea that they have always been in subjection, that their fathers lived in the same way; they will think they are obliged to suffer this evil, and will persuade themselves by example and imitation of others, finally investing those who order them around with proprietary rights, based on the idea that it has always been that way."[20]

This is why we launched the Financial Justice movement: to set people free by reminding them of their God-given rights and responsibilities as human beings to liberty and justice for all. Revolutionary Emiliano Zapata inspired millions of Mexican peasants by proclaiming, "It is better to die on your feet, than to live on your knees."[21]

Similarly, we believe it is better to chase dreams on your feet than to kill dreams on your knees. We believe net impact is even more valuable than net worth. We believe in getting free so we can help the next generation live free on their feet. A free people cannot be enslaved because every absolute power can survive only so long as the people consent.

La Boétie, again, said the people must "resolve to serve no more, and you are at once freed. I do not ask that you place hands upon the tyrant to topple him over, but simply that you support him no longer; then you will behold him, like a great Colossus whose pedestal has been pulled away, fall of his own weight and break in pieces."[20] It's time for the people, in other words, to withdraw our consent of the Financial Matrix and its plunder of our money. Just as water finds its own level, so too do political leaders rise or fall to the level of the people.

Imagine a united community of millions of entrepreneurs rising together, a group from all races, creeds, and ethnicities peacefully demanding Financial Justice for all. Naturally, a mass movement of this size will strengthen the backbone of political leaders. Eventually, Andrew Jackson–type political leaders will rise across the world to make ending the Financial Matrix and restoring Financial Justice a central election issue. (See Appendix I for details on how to replace the Financial Matrix with a free market banking and money system.)

This is our moonshot opportunity, and it can be yours as well: helping to bring Financial Justice to the world through the Life Super App and its leadership community.

Customers from all walks of life learn how to stop letting the Financial Matrix siphon money away from them. Once they realize its value, they then want to share the Super App with others, becoming members who build pipelines of happy customers. These pipelines provide ongoing income streams to help people move beyond merely blocking the Financial Matrix to breaking free from it.

This group of financially free B-business owners, who have built worldwide teams of customers and members taking small bites out of the Financial Matrix using the Super App, will grow into an unstoppable Financial Justice movement that no longer will tolerate financial enslavement. These free entrepreneurs will form, in La Boétie's words, "the vanguard of the revolutionary resistance movement against the despot. Through a process of educating the public to the truth, they will give back to the people knowledge of the blessings of liberty and of the myths and illusions fostered by the State."[20]

Everywhere people are yearning to live free. It is our responsibility not only to get free ourselves, but also to ensure the next generation has the opportunity to do so. We either support the Golden Rule Philosophy Free Market opportunity for all, or, by default, we support the Power Rule Philosophy force matrices for the chosen few. As for me and my family, we will follow the Golden Rule and strive to provide liberty and justice for all. The path to Financial Justice starts by joining the movement. The Super App begins the educational process to learn how to escape the Financial Matrix.

Every single person's actions matter. After all, just as an accumulation of snowflakes can cause a powerful avalanche, so too can an accumulation of free individuals cause an avalanche of freedom. We first set ourselves free to then help others remove their financial shackles. Freedom isn't free, and failure is not an option. By uniting freedom-loving people throughout the world, who are not beholden to the Financial Matrix, we provide answers to people groaning under economic oppression.

I do not want to sound overly dramatic, but if we do nothing, future generations will hold us accountable. When French Marshal Hubert Lyautey was serving in Africa, he once asked his gardener to plant a tree that provided foliage he enjoyed. The gardener explained that it would take nearly two hundred years for the tree to mature.

The marshal replied, "In that case, there is no time to lose. Plant it today."[19] Similarly, I wrote this book to start planting the seeds of financial truth today. We have no time to lose. The more we plant, the more these seeds will spread around the world, germinating into a reflowering of freedom. After all, every seed that takes root is one less person susceptible to Financial Matrix propaganda. This is our shot to end the Financial Matrix and restore Financial Justice. It's time to stand up and be counted. If not us, then who? If not now, then when?

The issue is always the same: the government or the market. There is no third solution.

—Ludwig von Mises

APPENDIX I

THE GOLDEN RULE FREE MARKET SOLUTION

The Financial Matrix is a force matrix with monopoly powers over the money and banking systems. It has inflated the money supply to previously unimaginable levels, has compounded debt levels to unmanageable levels, and still has not resolved the original systemic issue: the inherent instability of the fractional reserve banking money system leading to boom/bust business cycles.

Since the Financial Matrix received absolute power in 1971 with the termination of the gold standard, monetary challenges worldwide have compounded beyond anything previously experienced in history. As a result, any suggestion that gives even more power to the Financial Matrix is directionally incorrect. The solution is not to increase the size, power, and control of the force matrix; instead, the solution is to end the force matrix and replace it with the free market.

Although a book could be written on how the free market system applied to money and banking would end the Financial Matrix, for now let's zoom out to address the key steps and how they are interrelated. Fortunately, people do not have to understand all the technical minutiae of free market banking and money to play a part in the Financial Justice movement. However, I want to cover enough details so that anyone interested can do further research.

The first step is to end legal tender laws and state-mandated money. This allows the free market to determine what is money again, rather than the Financial Matrix. Real money is the most marketable commodity, and whether the market chooses precious metal money, Bitcoin (see Appendix II), or some other alternative, the key is that it is money chosen freely by the market, not coercively by the financial elites. Legitimate money, unlike today's fiat currency, is a store of value that endures, just as ancient Egypt's gold still has enduring value today. In contrast, no State fiat money system has ever survived, not even one of the many hundreds attempted.

The difference between real and fiat money is one has legitimate demand in the marketplace and the other is used only because the State coerces people to use it. The path to freedom must begin with the restoration of free market money by eliminating the central banks, the banking cartel, and the fraudulent FRB system, operating a free banking system under the general commercial laws other businesses must follow. This will reestablish free money in a free banking system with FRB permanently outlawed.

Central Banks vs. Free Banking

The second step is to end central banks designed to protect the fractional reserve banking system by creating fiat money, and thereby plundering the people. Vera Smith, in her thesis approved by Nobel Prize–winning Austrian economist Friedrich von Hayek, gave the classic definition of free banking as opposed to central banking:

A régime where note-issuing banks are allowed to set up in the same way as any other type of business enterprise, so long as they comply with the general company law. The requirement for their establishment is not special conditional authorization from a Government authority, but the ability to raise sufficient capital, and public confidence, to gain acceptance for their notes and ensure the profitability of the undertaking. Under such a system all banks would not only be allowed the same rights, but would also be subjected to the same responsibilities as other business enterprises. If they failed to meet their obligations they would be declared bankrupt and put into liquidation, and their assets used to meet the claims of their creditors, in which case the shareholders would lose the whole or part of their capital, and the penalty for failure would be paid, at least for the most part, by those responsible for the policy of the bank. . . . No bank would have the right to call on the Government or on any other institution for special help in time of need. No bank would be able to give its notes forced currency by declaring them to be legal tender for all payments. . . . A central bank, on the other hand, being founded with the aid either direct or indirect of the Government, is able to fall back on the Government for protection from the disagreeable consequences of its acts. The central bank, which cannot meet its obligations, is allowed to suspend payment . . . while its notes are given forced currency.[1]

Free Banking with 100% Reserves

Free banking is not a new concept. In fact, before central banks, there was much more competition among banks. Without competition, the banking system has been allowed to join forces in a cartel that benefits themselves at the people's expense. Free banking advocate Kevin Dowd noted:

> Free banking is—or at least ought to be—one of the key economic issues of our time. There is mounting evidence that the monetary instability created by the Federal Reserve—persistent and often erratic inflation, the unpredictable shifts of Federal Reserve monetary policy, and the gyrating interest rates that accompany both inflation and the monetary policy that creates it— have inflicted colossal damage on the US economy and on the fabric of American society more generally.[2]

Free banking, in other words, is free market competition in the banking field and breaks the central bank control over the money supply. This ensures the banks must compete to serve customers like other businesses must do. Ludwig von Mises explained in *Human Action*:"What is needed to prevent any further credit expansion is to place the banking business under the general rules of commercial and civil laws compelling every individual and firm to fulfill all obligations in full compliance with the terms of the contract."[3]

Whereas Mises emphasized the importance of bank competition under general commercial law, Murray Rothbard went one step further, suggesting that fractional reserve, since it is fraud against the consumer, should also be protected under the commercial code, explaining: "The answer to fraud, then, is not administrative regulation, but prohibition of tort and fraud under general law." By combining these two great economic minds' thinking, we arrive at free market banking with 100% mandated reserves operating under general commercial law. Mises explained the benefits of free banking over the fractional reserve system supported by central banks:

> Free banking is the only method available for the prevention of the dangers inherent in credit expansion. It would, it is true, not hinder a slow credit expansion, kept within very narrow limits, on the part of cautious banks which provide the public with all information required about their financial status. But under free banking it would have been impossible for credit expansion with all its inevitable consequences to have developed into a regular—one is tempted to say normal—feature of the economic system. Only free banking would have rendered the market economy secure against crises and depressions.[3]

Under the free market banking system, there would be no need for central banks because there would no longer be any FRB monetary instability that led to the boom/bust cycles in the first place. The banks would then compete and prosper by gaining the trust of customers and other banks to settle all customer transactions. Banks would be mandated not only to keep 100% money reserves on hand by law, but also to ensure they remain solvent.

After all, when one of their customers writes a large check to one of the customer's of a rival bank, the money reserve is moved from the first bank to the second bank. If the bank cannot make one of its customers checks good, then the bank has lost trust with its customers and other banks, not to mention it is now in legal trouble for violating the 100% reserve clause. Naturally, the free banking network would only do business with other banks with proven track records, and any bank suspected of fraudulent practices will have its banknotes, checks, and credit cards rejected by the other banks, similar to how businesses reject personal checks from suspected sources.

Trust is similarly the key ingredient with the bank's customers because, if customers suspect the bank of practicing FRB, they will demand their deposits back and seek a more trustworthy bank. A free market would punish banks for violating trust even before the government was aware FRB fraud was committed, and the misbehaving institutions would be essentially excommunicated from the banking profession.

Thus, FRB, for all practical purposes, would be eliminated under free banking competition, even without the 100% reserve requirement. However, like legal suspenders to go along with the free competition belt, even if some wily banker discovered a novel method of using fractional reserve banking, it's doubtful many bankers would risk prison sentences to do so. In 1994, after he had retired, former Federal Reserve Chair Paul Volcker, perhaps the most fiscally conservative person ever to hold the position, admitted:

> It is a sobering fact that the prominence of central banks in this century has coincided with a general tendency towards more inflation, not less. [I]f the overriding objective is price stability, we did better with the nineteenth-century gold standard and passive central banks, with currency boards, or even with "free

banking." The truly unique power of a central bank, after all, is the power to create money, and ultimately the power to create is the power to destroy.[4]

With free market banking and the end of central banks, however, the banks would then have to convince customers to forego access to their money in order to loan it to others. After all, in a free banking system, banks would make money by paying one interest rate to secure funds from depositors while charging a higher interest rate to loan out those same funds. In banking parlance, the idea is to *borrow short and lend long*.

Under a system such as the one just described, the money supply would not have expanded. This is because the depositor and borrower do not have access to the same money at the same time. Additionally, free banking would be much more efficient, performed at a fraction of the cost, and with reasonable instead of exorbitant profits because the banks would no longer be able to plunder the people.

Depositor money would always be secure (without the need for a central bank lender of last resort), the money supply would be stable (and selected by the free market), and inflation would be a thing of the past (banks no longer expanding the money supply). As such, the free-banking structure would allow banks to pursue whatever business ventures they deem profitable so long as they have 100% reserves to protect customer deposits.

Of course, this would legally be part of the general prohibition against fraud and breach of contract. Moreover, anyone would then be able to enter into the field of banking because it is one of the pillars of free markets. To do so, they must earn customer deposits by building trust. The interest rates on loans and securities would be determined by the supply and demand for money on the free market, which would then determine the market price (the market interest rate) of money.

Free banking would allow independent banks to open and close branches wherever they believed they could or couldn't compete effectively. Finally, there would be no need for FDIC insurance or any other excessive regulations since FRB is illegal, and the competition among banks would ensure that building trust would be the only way banks could stay in business. To compete, the banks would have to impress upon customers that their deposits were secure and impress upon competitive banking institutions that their banknotes were as good as gold.

Free banking is merely the consistent application of free market principles to money and banking. This would allow free people to enjoy the blessing of free markets to produce spiritual, political, and economic liberty. It is the total deregulation of the banking industry, which ensures each of the six free market pillars is followed within society. The free banking system would lead to the following benefits:

1. A free market money limited in supply
2. The end of FRB expansion of the money supply
3. Competition and innovation in the banking profession
4. No more central banks and their creation of fiat money out of thin air
5. Governments would have to budget because they could not borrow unlimited amounts of fiat money
6. No more inflation of the money supply
7. No more boom/bust business cycles
8. Banks would pay customers interest for saving money

9. Prosperity would increase for all producers
10. Financial manipulators could no longer unjustly profit from people's production
11. Rebirth of liberty
12. Reduced international meddling due to limited state funds

Free banking author Larry Sechrest concluded:

As long as money remains a tool of the state, that tool will continue to serve the state as a well-spring of income redistribution, social engineering, and military adventurism. A laissez-faire (Free Market) approach to money and banking is more than merely conducive to efficiency and stability. It is likely to prove to be the necessary precondition for prosperity, justice, and peace.[2]

It's not surprising that absolute power has destroyed every civilization where it existed because it behaves like the mythical spider monkeys. According to legend, spider monkeys are very difficult to hunt because they are quick, agile, and can leap from tree to tree. Thus, hunters developed an innovative way to capture them by walking through the jungle and dropping heavy jars.

These jars had narrow tops and wide bottoms. The hunters would place nuts, a spider monkey's favorite food, inside the jars. Eventually, the aroma would draw the curious critters to the jars. The tops of the jars were so narrow that the spider monkeys had to squeeze their hands inside. Once they grabbed the nuts, however, their fists became too large to remove through the small opening. Furthermore, the jar was too heavy for them to carry around.

They were effectively imprisoned by their own grip. Sure, the spider monkeys could regain their freedom by letting go of the free nuts, but they simply could not bring themselves to do so. In consequence, when the hunters returned, they not only gathered their jars with the nuts still inside, but also obtained dinner. The spider monkeys lost everything because they refused to let go of the free food.

Similarly, although the absolute power we've been calling the Financial Matrix believes it can create something out of nothing, the reality is the price is paid by the host economies until both the host and the parasite collapse. By restoring free market principles to money and banking, the Financial Matrix's absolute power will end. This would break up not only the Money power, but also the Media, Management, and Monopolies that we discussed earlier.

After all, the Financial Matrix is more than just a money monopoly (the only money source for the world), but after 1971, with the complete removal of the gold standard it became an absolute power. And just like the absolute power in the later Roman Empire, wherein all roads led to Rome, in the world economy all roads lead to the Financial Matrix. This is what led economist Joseph Stiglitz to conclude:"Rather than justice for all, we are evolving into a system of justice for those who can afford it. We have banks that are not only too big to fail, but too big to be held accountable."[5]

Imagine a world in which everything does not revolve around the Financial Matrix. Imagine Media with reasoned discussions on the pros and cons of all subjects, not just the ones sympatico with the Financial Matrix. This is what George

Orwell was emphasizing when he said, "Freedom of the Press, if it means anything at all, means the freedom to criticize and oppose."[6]

This is not possible if every opportunity for Media, Management, and Monopoly to advance means kissing the proverbial Financial Matrix ring in order to do so. Free markets would produce a free money and banking system that leads directly to a free press and educational system in which people could work without having to kowtow to a prevailing dogma.

Just as the Media cannot be freed from orbit until the Financial Matrix ends, neither can the nation-states. Democracy is not a guarantee of freedom, especially when one recalls that Hitler gained power democratically. In reality, no matter which party you vote for or how much they promise, the politicians must serve the absolute power of the Financial Matrix to even be viable candidates. Financial Matrix insider Carroll Quigley, a professor and mentor to Bill Clinton, admitted:

> The argument that the two parties should represent opposed ideals and policies . . . is a foolish idea. . . . Instead, the two parties should be almost identical, so that the American people can "throw the rascals out" at any election without leading to any profound or extensive shifts in policy.[7]

Moreover, democratic elections are one of the best tools used by the Financial Matrix to keep the people divided, as Ben Carson emphasized in an interview in 2020:

> Well, the reason it's called "One Nation" is because I want people to understand that we, the American

people, are not each other's enemies. The real enemies
are those people who are trying to divide us into every
little possible group. Any crack they drive a wedge into
to create, you know, gender wars, race wars, income
wars, age wars, any kind of war there is.[8]

Again, the focus must be on economically ending the Financial Matrix before we can politically fix the Management, including the controlled elections in which both parties now serve the
Financial Matrix. With a free market money and banking system,
along with a free press, we could then have free nation-states.
While I intend to write a complete proposal in my *And Justice for
All* book series, for now envision a federal government that is by
law allowed only a 10% import tax.

Furthermore, the federal government must no longer be
permitted to use its monopoly of force to give itself pay raises
(tax increases). All nation-states are monopolies of force. So
we should not be shocked that nation-states seek to increase
taxes (prices to citizens) since the point of all monopolies is
to increase prices to increase profits. Thus, the only protection
against this is to limit the federal government's taxes by law (import tax only).

Whereas bullets (war and disorder) and ballots (divided
democracies) favor the Financial Matrix's absolute power, budgets (limited governments) favor the people's liberty and justice.
Strangely, although every single household, business, and charity must budget limited funds, somehow the Financial Matrix
has convinced the people that political leaders should not be
held to the same standards. The quickest way to ensure balanced
budgets would be to mandate them. The problem isn't that the

leaders do not exist who can do this, but rather that people have not insisted this be done.

Furthermore, if the federal government needed more money, it would have to request the money from the fifty states' limited budgets. This would ensure that federal government spending would be reigned in because few politicians surrender money from their own budgets to fund another politician's budget. This would end one of the biggest problems in government—namely, the abuse of other people's money (namely, the taxpayers').

Incidentally, this is how every society that enjoyed limited government achieved it, and sadly, the reverse is how every society lost it. The old English parliaments kept the kings from having absolute power by limiting their access to unlimited funding. When the kings requested money, they had to negotiate and compromise with parliament in a win-win fashion; otherwise, the kings received no new funds. Today, our federal government can borrow unlimited funds from the Federal Reserve, which simply creates it out of thin air.

Then the representatives from the fifty states, instead of restraining the federal government, get in line to beg for free money, all paid for by ever-growing federal deficits. This is a far cry from the freedom-loving immigrants who came to America to escape oppressive force matrices.

Finally, by removing the Financial Matrix's absolute power over Money, Media, Management, and Monopolies, the excess profits and taxes would be returned to the people. The Monopolies would naturally fall because there would no longer be an absolute power nation-state to set and enforce regulations that create them. The free market system would reign within the economies of the world, and the people would be set free.

Imagine a world not being destroyed by spider monkey absolute power.

Imagine one without income, Social Security, death, and sales taxes. I haven't lost my mind, and not only is this mathematically possible, but before the advent of the Federal Reserve in 1913, it was policy reality in America. The reason America was the freest, most prosperous, and fastest growing nation in the world was because it did not have oppressive taxation, massive debts, or rampant inflation. Immigrants from all over the world sought these shores to enjoy more freedom and opportunity than were available anywhere else. If such a free and prosperous society sounds crazy today, then that is proof of just how effective Financial Matrix propaganda has been at convincing us that our heavy tax and debt burden is not only somehow normal, but necessary.

Tax Revenue

Taxes (including social contributions) as a share of national income.

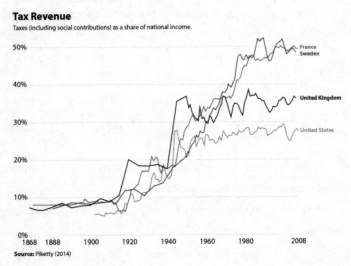

Source: Piketty (2014)

The tax revenue graphic displays what the total taxes were at the end of the nineteenth century and what they are today at the beginning of the twenty-first century. Total taxation tripled in fifty years after the Federal Reserve was formed, and this is before the effects of debt and inflation are added into the equation.

If these free market strategies were to once again be implemented, the private sector would explode with new businesses, new jobs, and new private sector charities, without the weight of massive debts, taxes, and inflation. Even with each state and locality setting its own taxes, the people would be protected because the competition among states and localities would ensure taxes do not turn into plunder.

After all, if a state taxes too much, the people can vote with their feet and move, punishing the offending state with lost revenue until it wises up (much as is happening in California as I write this). Finally, without an absolute state, the monopolies supported by the nation-state would be defunded and deregulated. The GRP Free Market would do the rest, and companies would rise and fall depending on how well they serve customers. These measures would end the Financial Matrix, restore Financial Justice, and restore freedom and prosperity to all.

Bitcoin is a technological tour de force.

—Bill Gates

APPENDIX II

FREE MARKET MONEY—
GOLD VS. BITCOIN

Bitcoin is a decentralized, distributed, digital virtual currency created in 2009 as a direct result of the housing market crash and has been called analogous to digital gold. It was created by the pseudonymous Satoshi Nakamoto and follows the protocols outlined in the white paper released at its creation. The identity of the person or persons who created the technology is still a mystery to this day.

Bitcoin offers the promise of lower transaction fees than traditional online payment mechanisms and is operated by a decentralized, distributed authority, unlike the Financial Matrix's centrally issued currencies. Since bitcoins are digital, there are no physical coins, only balances on a public ledger transparently displayed with the transaction history. Furthermore, since bitcoins are decentralized and are not issued or backed by any government or bank, no entity can control the creation, transfer, or value of them. Instead, bitcoins have market price because, like all goods and services, the market values them.

In fact, the value appears to be growing as people realize the size of the con the Financial Matrix is perpetrating at their expense. Bitcoin, essentially, is a grassroots movement aimed at the creation of free market money, entirely separate from centralized governments and force matrices.

The idea of free market money is not new. Also, the idea of digital money is not new. And certainly, the desire for stable money goes back as far as money itself. The reason Bitcoin is so revolutionary is that it figured out elegant solutions to massive age-old problems in order to accomplish all of these desires for money in one invention. One of the biggest obstacles to creating something like Bitcoin was the problem often referred to as the Byzantine Generals Problem (BGP). Software entrepreneur Marc Andreessen described this:

> Bitcoin is the first practical solution to a longstanding problem in computer science called the Byzantine Generals Problem (BGP). To quote from the original paper defining the BGP: "[Imagine] a group of generals of the Byzantine army camped with their troops around an enemy city. Communicating only by messenger, the generals must agree upon a common battle plan. However, one or more of them may be traitors who will try to confuse the others. The problem is to find an algorithm to ensure that the loyal generals will reach agreement." [1]

The BGP, in other words, poses how to identify trustworthy actions from fraudulent ones, and establish a basis for trust in a decentralized network of unrelated parties like the Internet.

Nakamoto's technological solution created, for the first time in world history, the ability to transfer value between distant peoples without relying on a trusted intermediary, as neither banks nor governments are needed to successfully complete the transaction. Indeed, the ramifications of Bitcoin's core technologies are so profound that it has rightfully been suggested that

Nakamoto is a worthy potential recipient of both the Nobel Prize for economics and the Turing Award for advances in computer science. The four fundamental technologies uniquely encapsulated to create Bitcoin are:

1. **Digital Signatures:** These ensure identities cannot be forged, permitting one party to securely verify transactions with other parties.

2. **Peer-to-Peer Networks:** Durable networks like BitTorrent or TCP/IP are difficult to take down and require no trusted central third party.

3. **Proof-of-Work:** This ensures users cannot spend the same money twice, even without a central authority to regulate transactions. Bitcoin has created an incentive system for *miners,* who are paid by *discovering* new coins, by running powerful networks of computers that validate transactions, securing them from tampering. Moreover, anyone with computational resources can anonymously and democratically choose to become a miner to earn new coins.

4. **Distributed Ledger:** Bitcoin records the history of each and every transaction in every wallet. This *blockchain* ledger publicly displays all validated transactions.

Essential Characteristics of Money

These technological innovations created Bitcoin with the essential characteristics of money, money that is scarce (only twenty-one million bitcoins will ever be created), durable (being digital, they don't degrade), portable (the digital signature allows bitcoins to travel with you anywhere and to be transmitted electronically), divisible (into trillionths called satoshis), verifiable (through the public blockchain), easy to store (paper or electronic), fungible (each bitcoin is equal in value), difficult to counterfeit (cryptographically impossible), and achieving widespread acceptance within the marketplace, with many top technologists and programmers working overtime to improve it. The following chart from MAXIMALIST indicates how Bitcoin stacks up to other potential moneys.

Traits of Money	Gold	Fiat	Bitcoin	"Crypto"
Fungible (Interchangeable)	High	High	High	High
Non-Consumable	High	High	High	High
Portability	Moderate	High	High	High
Durable	High	Moderate	High	Moderate
Highly Divisible	Moderate	Moderate	High	High
Secure (Cannot be counterfeited)	Moderate	Moderate	High	Moderate
Easily Transactable	Low	High	High	Moderate
Scarce (Predictable Supply)	Moderate	Low	High	Moderate
Sovereign (Government Issued)	Low	High	Low	Low
Decentralized	Low	Low	High	Low
Smart (Programmable)	Low	Low	High	Low

Source: Best Bitcoin Buyers Maximalist

Money, according to economist William Stanley Jevons, becomes money by progressing through four particular stages:

1. **Collectible:** First, people collect the item because it has a peculiar and special value to them—that is, they may like the way the shells, beads, or precious metals look and feel, choosing to save the items of interest.

2. **Store of value:** Soon enough, people demand that the peculiar item will be recognized as an acceptable means of keeping and storing value. The more people recognize the perceived value of the former

collectible, the more purchasing power increases as more people begin collecting it as a store of value, until a plateau of stored value is reached.

3. **Medium of exchange:** Now, the new money is fully recognized as a store of value, and its purchasing power has stabilized, thus making it a suitable medium of exchange. Interestingly, the famous story of the man who traded ten thousand bitcoins (approximately $100 million in bitcoins today) for several pizzas indicates that the four-step money progression was not clearly understood, pushing the new collectible into a medium of exchange before its monetary value had plateaued and significantly overpaying for those pizzas.

4. **Unit of account:** The last stage of money progression is when money becomes widely used as the medium of exchange and all other goods and services are priced in terms of the new money. Bitcoins, for instance, are not at this stage yet because items purchased with bitcoins are just the dollar price charged by the merchant and then converted into bitcoin terms at the current market exchange rate. Indeed, bitcoins will not become the unit of account until merchants accept bitcoins for payment without regard to bitcoins' exchange rate against other currencies.[2]

Bitcoin is currently progressing from a collectible to a legitimate store of value, and the world is witnessing the birth of a potentially new free market money. Naturally, it will take years to progress from a store of value to a true medium of exchange, and the path is unpredictable; however, the speed at which the dollar and other fiat currencies are inflating could cause Bitcoin to progress faster than most people think.

Historically, the progression from a store of value to a medium of exchange took gold many centuries, and since a new money is not a common occurrence, no one can accurately predict how all of this will play out. What is known, at this point, is Bitcoin has progressed from a techno-cyberpunk collectible to an established store of value worldwide, a value that increased significantly in its first decade of life.

As already mentioned, Bitcoin is limited to a grand total of twenty-one million bitcoins, all displayed on the blockchain's public ledger. Unlike the Federal Reserve fiat money system, this limits the total supply, and anyone attempting to fraudulently duplicate bitcoins will be rejected on the blockchain. The key point of monetary theory, discussed in the book several times, is how Bitcoin has solved the metaphysical-to-physical fraud. In an impressive digital fashion, Bitcoin has linked the metaphysical and physical aspects together programmatically.

It is impossible for fraudsters to create metaphysical titles of bitcoins and pass them off as legitimate. After all, the miner network displays the ledger, publicly showing who actually owns the bitcoin. The digital bitcoins, in other words, are not physical at all, and since they are metaphysically limited, the Financial Matrix is unable to fraudulently expand the metaphysical titles.

ACKNOWLEDGMENTS

While writing demands many hours alone to study, think, and build the materials into a rough draft, the final product can only be achieved through a team effort. Fortunately, I am surrounded by a world-class team, one that is as committed to the Financial Justice movement, and this book, as I am.

A great team begins at home and I was blessed to marry up. Laurie Woodward is lovely, loving, and loyal, to name just a few of her superb qualities. Her willingness to go the extra mile on nearly every aspect of our lives gave me the time necessary to take on a project of this magnitude. She never complained about the extra workload; she never criticized her husband's reclusive behavior; and she never wavered in her support, despite her and our four adult children (Jordan, Christina, Lance, and Jeremiah) being subjected to my Financial Matrix ramblings weekly during our family call. If it were not for Laurie's continual belief, encouragement, and support, this book would never have seen the light of day.

The second part of this team is my lifetime friendship and business partnership with Chris Brady. I cannot fathom writing this book without his input. Not only did he read every word in the manuscript, but he took "providing feedback" to a whole new level. Sure, he suggested edits to nearly every paragraph to ensure I said clearly what I intended to say, but he also challenged any assumptions arrived at without sufficient logical/factual support. As a result, he forced me to connect dots in a step-by-step fashion to help the readers think through the issues for themselves. He even proposed sentence rewrites when his friend's writing became overly verbose. For the CEO of a multimillion dollar company to dedicate hours per day for months to improve this book, without complaint, reward, or fanfare, makes me forever in his debt.

Another key aspect in completing the book was the efforts of Marc and Kristine Militello. Kristine is not only a former English teacher, but is an artist of the written word. Her ability to read a paragraph, feel what it communicates, and then quickly ascertain what, if anything, is missing, is a sixth sense. Sometimes the edits were a few words, other times it was complete rewrite to simplify the topic, but when completed, the work was greatly improved because of her gift. Afterward, Marc went through the entire manuscript to identify quotes that needed footnoting, and then verified the source of each. Without the countless hours cheerfully invested by these two, this book would not be the same.

In addition, I would like to thank the Life community for sharing their stories of financial challenges caused by the Financial Matrix. It is because of your inspiration that the Financial Justice movement was born. I would also like to give a special shout out to Pastor Scott VanderPloeg, whose Biblical insights on money and work helped clarify my thinking on the Financial Matrix, while his constant encouragement helped me press to the finish line. Furthermore, I would like to thank the corporate staff at Life. COO Rob Hallstrand and his team, including Steve Kendall, Jordan Woodward, and Kristen Sherman, are a joy to work with and turned this book around in record time.

Finally, none of this would have been possible except for the love and mercy of my Lord and Savior Jesus Christ. To Him be all the glory and honor!

NOTES

Prologue

1. *The Matrix*. The Wachwoski Brothers. Burbank, CA: Warner Bros., 1999.
2. Burke, Edmond. Open Culture, March 13, 2016. www.openculture.com/2016/03/edmund-burke-on-in-action.html.
3. Fuller, Buckminster. *A Fuller View*. Studio City, CA: Michael Wiese Productions, 2012.

Chapter 1

1. Pound, Ezra. "Seven Quotes from Ezra Pound." Exploring Your Mind, March 30, 2020. www.exploringyourmind.com/seven-quotes-from-ezra-pound/.
2. *Report on the Economic Well-Being of U.S. Households in 2019*. Federal Reserve, May 2020. www.federal-reserve.gov/publications/files/2019-report-eco-nomic-well-being-us-households-202005.pdf.
3. Butler, James. *Total US Debt Soars to Nearly $60trn, Foreshadows New Recession. RT Question More.* June 16, 2014. www.rt.com/usa/166352-us-to-tal-debt-sixty-trillion/#:~:text=Total%20debt%20(the%20combination%20of,(IVN)%20op%2Ded.

4. Issa, Erin El. *2019 American Household and Credit Card Study*. NerdWallet, Inc, 2020. www.nerdwallet.com/blog/average-credit-card-debt-household/.

5. Carter, Joe. *6 Quote: PJ O'Rourke on Government and Politics. Action Institute Power Blog. March 4, 2019*

6. Hazlit, Henry. *Economics in One Lesson*. Auburn, AL: Mises Institute, 1946.

7. Radin, Charles A. *Business Cycle Expansions and Contractions*. National Bureau of Economic Research, 2020. www2.nber.org/cycles/.

8. *Annual Statistical Supplement, 2019*. Ssa.gov. www.ssa.gov/policy/docs/statcomps/supplement/.

9. Flamm, Matthew Caleb. "George Santayana." Internet Encyclopedia of Philosophy. www.iep.utm.edu/santayan/.

10. Einstein, Albert. Goodreads.com. www.goodreads.com/quotes/76863-compound-interest-is-the-eighth-wonder-of-the-world-he.

11. "The Explosive Effect of Compound Interest." Live-Counter.com, 2020. www.live-counter.com/compound-interest/.

12. Julavitis, Rob, and Sarah Kerr. "Retirees Live a 20th Century Retirement in the 21st Century, Wells Fargo Survey Finds." Wells Fargo, October 18, 2019. newsroom.wf.com/English/news-releases/news-release-details/2019/Retirees-Live-a-20th-Century-Retirement-in-the-21st-Century-Wells-Fargo-Survey-Finds/

13. American Psychological Association. *Stress in America: Paying with our Health*. APA, 2015. www.apa.org/news/press/releases/stress/2014/stress-report.pdf.

Chapter 2

1. Weatherford, Jack. *History of Money*. New York: Three Rivers Press, 1997.
2. "Credit River Case." Minnesota State Law Library, 1969. www.mn.gov/law-library/legal-topics/cred-it-river-case.jsp.
3. Rothbard, Murray N. *The Mystery of Banking*. New York: Richardson, Snyder, Ditton, 1983.
4. Richardson, George P. *Feedback Thought in Social Science and Systems Theory*. UK: Pegasus, 1999.
5. Kolko, Gabriel. *The Triumph of Conservatism*. New York: Simon and Schuster, 2008.

Chapter 3

1. Rothbard, Murray. *The History of Money and Banking: Colonial Era–WWII*. Auburn, AL: Ludwig Von Mises Institute, 2002.
2. "Bank Failures During the Great Depression." The Great Depression, 2020. www.thegreatdepressioncauses.com/great-depression/banks.
3. Weatherford, Jack. *History of Money*. New York: Three Rivers Press, 1997.
4. Senge, Peter. *The Fifth Discipline*. New York: Currency-Double Day, 1990.
5. Hayek, F. A. *The Road to Serfdom*. UK: Routledge and Sons, 1944.
6. "What Caused the Great Depression." Foundation for Economic Education, February 2, 2018. www.fee.org/articles/what-caused-the-great-depression/.

7.   Hazlitt, Henry. *Economics in One Lesson*. New York: Harper & Bros, 1946.

8.   Bourne, Randolph. *The State and Other Essays*. UK: Christie Books, 2016.

9.   Shirduth, Ramphal, Shridath S. "Sovereign Default: A Backwards Glance." *Third World Quarterly*, Vol. II, 2007.

10. Mises, Ludwig von. *The Causes of the Economic Crisis*. Auburn, AL: Ludwig von Mises Institute, 2006.

11. Mises, Ludwig Von. *The Threat of Money and Credit*. New York: Skyhorse Publishing, 2013.

12. *The Financial Crisis Inquiry Report: Final Report of the National Commission on the Causes of the Financial and Economic Crisis in the United States*. The Financial Crisis Inquiry Commission, January 2011. www.fcic-static.law.stanford.edu/cdn_media/fcic-reports/fcic_final_report_full.pdf.

13. Yellen, Janet. CNBC [video], April 6, 2020. www.cnbc.com/video/2020/04/06/watch-cnbcs-full-interview-with-former-fed-chair-janet-yellen.html.

14. Martens, Pam, and Russ Martens. "The Fed Does Not Ride to the Rescue of Wall Street Yesterday: What's Up?" Wall Street on Parade, September 9, 2020. www.wallstreetonparade.com/2020/09/the-fed-does-not-ride-to-the-rescue-of-wall-street-yesterday-whats-up/.

15. Hegel, Georg. Goodreads.com.

16. Powell, Jerome. *60 Minutes*. CBS News [video], May 17, 2020. www.cbsnews.com/news/full-transcript-fed-chair-jerome-powell-60-minutes-interview-economic-recovery-from-coronavirus-pandemic.

17. Acton, Lord. Online Library of Liberty. Liberty-fund.org/quotes/214.

18. Senge, Peter. *The Fifth Discipline*. New York: Currency-Double Day, 1990.

19. Quigley, Carroll. *Tragedy and Hope*. New York: Macmillan, 1966.

Chapter 4

1. Bastiat, Frédéric. *The Law*. Auburn, AL: Ludwig von Mises Institute, 2007.

2. Boétie, Étienne de La. *The Politics of Obedience: The Discourse of Voluntary Servitude*. Auburn, AL: Ludwig von Mises Institute, 2015.

3. Solzhenitsyn, Aleksandr *The Gulag Archipelago*. New York: Harper and Row, 1973.

4. Rand, Ayn, et al. *Capitalism: The Unknown Ideal*. Chapter 6 *Gold & Economic Freedom;* Alan Greenspan. New York: New American Library, 1966.

5. Rothbard, Murray. *The History of Money and Banking: Colonial Era—WWll;* Introduction by Joseph Salerno. Auburn, AL: Ludwig von Mises Institute, 2002.

6. Grim, Ryan. "Priceless: How the Federal Reserve Bought the Economics Profession." HuffPost, May 13, 2013. www.huffpost.com/entry/priceless-how-the-federal_n_278805.

7. Auerbach, Robert D. *Deception and Abuse at the Fed*. Austin: University of Texas Press, 2008.

8. Lippman, Walter. *Opinion*. San Diego: Harcourt, 1922.

9.   Chomsky, Noam. *Media Control.* New York: Seven Stories Press, 1991.

10. Bagdikian, Ben. *The New Media Monopoly.* Boston: Beacon Press, 1983.

11. Solomon, Norman. *Cover of Media Mergers.* Quote by Mark Crispin Miller. www.niemanreports.org/ articles/coverage-of-media-mergers/.

12. Wormser, René A. *Foundations: Their Power and Influence.* New York: Devin-Adair Company, 1958.

13. Bernays, Edward. *Propaganda.* Brooklyn, New York: Ig Publishing, 1928.

14. Chomsky, Noam. "On the State of the Nation, Iraq and the Election." *Democracy Now*, October 21, 2004. www.chomsky.info/20041021/.

15. Sutton, Antony C. *National Suicide: Military Aid to the Soviet Union.* New Rochelle, NY: Arlington House, 1973.

16. Mackenzie, Debora, and Andy Coghlan. "Revealed—The Capitalist Network that Runs the World." *New Scientist*, October 19, 2011. www.new-scientist.com/article/mg21228354-500-revealed-the-capitalist-network-that-runs-the-world/.

17. Howe, Frédéric C. *The Confessions of a Monopolist.* Chicago: Public Publishing Co., 1906.

18. Schumpeter, Joseph A. *Capitalism, Socialism and Democracy.* New York: Harper Perennial, 1950.

19. Kolko, Gabriel. *The Triumph of Conservatism.* New York: Simon and Schuster, 2008.

20. Bastiat, Frédéric. *The Law.* Auburn, AL: Ludwig von Mises Institute, 2007.

21. Butler, Smedley D. *War Is a Racket.* Los Angeles, CA: Feral House, 1935.

22. CNN [article], April 4, 2012. www.cnn.com/inter-active/2012/04/us/table.military.troops/.

Chapter 5

1. Augustine. *The City of God*. Peabody, MA: Hendrickson Publishers, 2009.

2. Mises, Ludwig von. *Omnipotent Government*. New Haven, CT: Yale University Press, 1944.

3. Nock, Albert Jay. *Our Enemy the State*. North Stratford, NH: Ayer Publishing Co., 1972.

4. Oppenheimer, Franz. *The State*. New York: B. W. Huebsch Publishing, 1992.

5. Jouvenel, Bertrand de. *The Ethics of Redistribution*. New York: Cambridge University Press, 1951.

6. Rochefoucauld, Francois de la. *Reflections or Sentences and Moral Maxims*. West Roxbury, MA: B & R Samizdat Express, 2009.

7. Marx, Karl. *Critique of the Gotha Program*. Wildside Press, 1891.

8. Spencer, Herbert. *The Man versus the State*. New York: D. Appleton and Company, 1885.

9. Luntz, Frank. "Snapchat Generation Is Ignoring the GOP." *Times Herald*, March 14, 2016.

10. Maltsev, Yuri N. "Mass Murder and Public Slavery." A *Journal of Political Economy*, vol. 22, no.2, Fall 2017.

11. Smith, Marion. "Socialism Is Slavery." Victims of Communism Memorial Foundation, May 1, 2018. www.victimsofcommunism.org/socialism-slavery/.

12. Bloom, Allan. *The Changing of the American Mind.* New York: Simon and Schuster, 1987.

13. Sutton, Antony C. (taken from web page): "The Best Enemies Money Can Buy" [video], 1980.

14. Hugo, Victor. Goodreads.com.

15. Nock, Albert Jay. *Memoirs of a Superfluous Man.* Auburn, AL: Ludwig von Mises Institute, 2016.

16. Opitz, Edmund. "Biblical Roots of American Liberty." Foundation for Economic Education, July 1991.

17. Boaz, David. *The Libertarian Mind.* New York: Simon and Schuster, 1997.

18. Smith, Adam. *The Invisible Hand.* UK: Penguin, 1997.

19. I Thessalonians 3:10 (King James).

20. Paine, Thomas. *Common Sense.* UK: Penguin, 1982.

21. Mises, Ludwig von. *Bureaucracy.* Indianapolis, IN: Liberty Fund, 2007.

22. Opitz, Edmund. "The Declaration of Independence Against Itself." Foundation for Economic Education.

23. King, Martin Luther, Jr. *The Essential Martin Luther King Jr.: I Have a Dream and Other Essential Writings.* Boston, MA: Beacon Press, 2013.

24. Lewis, C. S. *The Abolition of Man.* New York: Harper Collins, 2009.

25. Mangalwadi, Vishal. *The Book that Made Your World: How the Bible Created the Soul of Western Civilization.* Nashville, TN: Thomas Nelson, 2011.

Chapter 6

1. Guzzardo, George. *Torch of Freedom*. Cary, NC: Obstacles Press, 2016.

2. *Braveheart*. Santa Monica, CA: Icon Entertainment International, 1995.

3. Henry, Patrick. Libertytree.ca.

4. King, Martin Luther, Jr. *The Essential Martin Luther King Jr.: I Have a Dream and Other Essential Writings*. Boston, MA: Beacon Press, 2013.

5. Tolstoy, Leo. *Anna Karenina*. UK: Penguin, 2000.

6. Hayek, F. A. *The Road to Serfdom*. UK: Routledge and Sons, 1944.

7. Erhard, Ludwig. "Architect of a Miracle." Foundation for Economic Education.

8. Senge, Peter. *The Fifth Discipline*. New York: Currency-Double Day, 1990.

9. Fuller, Buckminster. *A Fuller View*. Studio City, CA: Michael Wiese Productions, 2012.

10. Sinek, Simon. *Start with Why*. New York: Penguin, 2009.

Chapter 7

1. Schwab, Charles. *Invested*. Westminster, MD: Penguin Random House, 2019.

2. Mineo, Liz. "To Age Better, Eat Better." *Harvard Gazette*, May, 3, 2017. www.news.harvard.edu/gazette/story/2017/05/much-of-life-is-beyond-our-control-but-dining-smartly-can-help-us-live-healthier-longer/.

3. *How Does High DHA Fish Oil Affect Health? A Systematic Review of Evidence.* March 1, 2018 www. pubmed.ncbi.nlm.nih.gov/29494205/

4. MD News. Special Feature. June 2008.

5. Kiyosaki, Robert. *Cashflow Quadrant.* New York: Tech Press, 1998.

6. Covey, Stephen R. *The 7 Habits of Highly Successful People.* New York: Simon and Schuster, 1989.

7. Gerber, Michael. *E-myth Revisited.* New York: Harper Collins, 2004.

8. Beughin, Jacques. *A New Way to Measure Word-of-Mouth Marketing,* April 1, 2010 www.mckinsey. com/business-functions/marketing-and-sales/ our-insights/a-new-way-to-measure-word-of-mouth-marketing#.

9. Godin, Seth. *Unleashing the Ideavirus.* New York: Simon & Schuster, 2000.

10. Getty, J. Paul. Inspiringquotes.us.

Chapter 8

1. Fuller, Buckminster. *A Fuller View.* Studio City, CA: Michael Wiese Productions, 2012.

2. Reid, Carlton. "How the Bicycle Beats Evolution and How Steve Jobs Was So Taken with This Fact." *Bike Boom [blog],* March 14, 2015. www.bike-boom.info/efficiency/.

3. Jones, Charles Edward. *Life Is Tremendous.* Boiling Springs, PA: Tremendous Leadership, 1968.

4. Tan, Chee-Seng *Openness to Experience Enhances Creativity* www.onlinelibrary.wiley.com/doi/abs/10.1002/jocb.170.

5. Elkins, Kathleen. "11 Things to Give Up if You Want to Be a Millionaire" CNBC, May 11, 2017. www.cnbc.com/2017/05/11/things-to-give-up-if-you-want-to-be-a-millionaire.html.

6. Buffett, Warren. CNBC. March 27th, 2018 www.google.com/amp/s/www.cnbc.com/amp/2018/03/27/warren-buffetts-key-tip-for-success-read-500-pages-a-day.html.

7. Elkins, Kathleen. "Berkshire Hathaway Star Followed Warren Buffett's Advice: Read 500 Pages a Day." CNBC, March 27, 2017. www.cnbc.com/2018/03/27/warren-buffetts-key-tip-for-success-read-500-pages-a-day.html

8. Rohn, Jim. Goodreads.com.

9. Walton, Sam. *Made in America.* New York: Bantam Books, 1993.

10. Senge, Peter. *The Fifth Discipline.* New York: Currency-Double Day, 1990.

11. Carnegie, Dale. *How to Win Friends and Influence People.* New York: Pocket Books, 1936.

12. Gerber, Michael. *E-Myth Revisited.* New York: Harper Collins, 1995.

13. Waitley, Denis. Goodreads.com.

14. Muhammad, Ali. Goodreads.com.

15. Covey, Stephen. Goodreads.com.

16. Disney, Walt. Goodreads.com.

17. Hawkins, Dan. *Swing: The Courage to Become.* Cary, NC: Obstacles Press, 2017.

18. Standridge, Jordan. "Putin Can't Stop the Gospel." The Cripplegate, July 19, 2016. www.thecripple-gate.com/putin-cant-stop-the-gospel/.

19. Grant, George. *The Micah Mandate*. Nashville, TN: Cumberland House, 1995.

Chapter 9

1. "Semmelweis' Germ Theory." Explorable.com, August 21, 2010. www.explorable.com/semmel-weis-germ-theory.

2. Kuhn, Thomas. *The Structure of Scientific Revolutions*. Chicago: University of Chicago Press, 1996.

3. Schopenhauer, Arthur. Goodreads.com.

4. Hayek, Friedrich, August von. Azquotes.com.

5. Greenspan, Alan. *There is No Other Agency . . .* [video] www.bitchute.com/video/cYFueyo9Vmeh/.

6. De, Nikhilesh. "US Fed Chair Says Private Entities Shouldn't help Design Central Bank Digital Currencies." Coindesk, June 17, 2020. www.coindesk.com/us-fed-chair-says-private-entities-should-not-help-design-central-bank-digital-currencies.

7. Weaver, Richard M. *Ideas Have Consequences*. Chicago: University of Chicago Press, 1948.

8. Rothbard, Murray J. *The Austrian Theory of the Trade Cycle and Other Essays*. Auburn, AL: Ludwig con Mises Institute, 1983.

9. Jefferson, Thomas. Goodreads.com.

10. Dilorenzo, Thomas J. *Hamilton's Curse*. New York: Three Rivers Press, 2008.

11. Rothbard, Murray J. *Egalitarianism as a Revolt Against Nature*. Auburn, AL: Ludwig von Mises Institute. 2000.

12. Schlesinger, Arthur M. *The Age of Jackson*. New York: Little, Brown Publishing, 1945.

13. Biddle, Nicholas. *Nicholas Biddle Papers*. Library of Congress. www.lccn.loc.gov/mm78012690.

14. Hammond, Bray. "Jackson's Fight with the 'Money Power'." *American Heritage*, June 1956. www.americanheritage.com/jacksons-fight-money-power.

15. Brands, H. W. *Andrew Jackson: His Life and Times*. New York: Anchor Books, 2005.

16. North, Gary. "Defenders of Crony Capitalism: Why Historians Ridicule Andrew Jackson." August 13, 2016. www.garynorth.com/HistoriansJackson.pdf.

17. Heller, Mikhail, and Nekrich, Aleksandr. *Utopia in Power: The History of the Soviet Union*. Summit Publishing, 1988.

18. Orwell, George. *Shooting an Elephant and Other Essays*. UK: Secker and Warburg, 1950.

19. Hutchins, Robert M. *The Great Conversation: The Substance of a Liberal Education*. Chicago: William Benton Publishing, 1952.

20. Boétie, Étienne de La. *Politics of Obedience: The Discourse of Voluntary Servitude*. Auburn, AL: Ludwig von Mises Institute, 2015.

21. Zapata, Emiliano. Goodreads.com.

APPENDIX I

1. Smith, Vera C. *The Rationale of Central Banking and the Free Banking Alternative.* Indianapolis, IN: Liberty Fund, 1990.

2. Sechrest, Larry. *Free Banking: Theory, History and a Laissez-Faire Model.* Auburn, AL: Ludwig von Mises Institute, 2008.

3. Mises, Ludwig von. *Human Action.* Auburn, AL: Ludwig von Mises Institute, 1999.

4. Volcker, Paul. January 18, 2014. www.centralbanking.com/central-banking-journal/feature/2321715/lifetime-achievement-award-paul-volcker.

5. Stilglitz, Joseph E. "Justice for Some." Project Syndicate, November 4, 2010. www.project-syndicate.org/commentary/justice-for-some?barrier=-accesspaylog.

6. Orwell, George. *Shooting an Elephant and Other Essays.* UK: Secker and Warburg, 1950.

7. Quigley, Carroll. *Tragedy and Hope: A History of the World in Our Time.* New York: Macmillan, 1966.

8. Carson, Ben. MSNBC [video], May 21, 2014.

APPENDIX II

1. Andreessen, Marc. "Why Bitcoin Matters." New York Times, January 21, 2014. dealbook.nytimes.com/2014/01/21/why-bitcoin-matters/.

2. Jevons, William Stanley. *The Theory of Political Economy.* New York: MacMillan and Co., 1871.

ORRIN WOODWARD

Originally a systems engineer with a degree from Kettering University, four patents, and a national benchmarking award, Woodward became a cofounder and Chairman of Life, and a *New York Times* best-selling author with over 1 million books sold in nine languages. He also held a GUINNESS WORLD RECORD for the Largest Book Signing, is one of the Top 20 Most Followed Leadership Influencers on Twitter, is ranked on *Inc. Magazine's* Top 50 Leadership and Management Experts, and its Top 100 Speakers list.